C000301636

ARE YOU ALL RIGHT, DADDY?

Philip Woolcock

MINERVA PRESS
LONDON
MIAMI DELHI SYDNEY

ARE YOU ALL RIGHT, DADDY?
Copyright © Philip Woolcock 2000

All Rights Reserved

No part of this book may be reproduced in any form
by photocopying or by any electronic or mechanical means,
including information storage or retrieval systems,
without permission in writing from both the copyright
owner and the publisher of this book.

ISBN 075411 149 0

First Published 2000 by
MINERVA PRESS
315–317 Regent Street
London W1R 7YB

Printed in Great Britain for Minerva Press

ARE YOU ALL RIGHT, DADDY?

For Shelley & family
with love

Philip Woodward

For Judy, Sam, Barney and of course, Uncle Chris

Acknowledgement

Valerie Beck for her proof reading and helpful suggestions and Robin Chadwick and family for their encouragement and support during the writing of this book, Trinity the Hospice in the Fylde and The Children and Adolescent Oncology Ward, Christie Hospital, Manchester.

Photographs reproduced by kind permission of The *Gazette*, Blackpool.

Chapter One

I felt both exhilarated and a little sad as I watched her disappear into the back of the green Jaguar. My mind raced through the terrible events that had brought us together on that thundery afternoon. My daughter, Louise, was standing at my right shoulder deep in thought. As Diana closed the car door she looked up towards our third floor window and smiled. Louise lifted her right hand and Diana returned her wave. As she did so the car and motorcade pulled slowly away. I looked at Louise: she was smiling wistfully and gazing at the crowd in the square below. The Princess of Wales had come into our lives for the first time. Little did I know at that time that she would return one year later under very different circumstances.

Louise had arrived in the world on a wing and a prayer, three pounds twelve ounces of jaundiced, wrinkled humanity. Feebly clutching at air, twisting and staring into the middle distance in numb surprise. She was not expected to survive the night, having taken everybody by surprise on that cold spring evening. She had not been due to arrive until the summer. After a few days the doctors had said that she would live, and one by one her plethora of life-giving tubes was removed and she began to lose her wrinkled appearance and pale yellow complexion. By the time she came home three weeks later she resembled a pretty pixie.

As a young parent I felt a combination of great pride and joy, but also fear. I found it difficult to comprehend the enormity of my responsibility. Such thoughts were quite quickly dispelled by the feeling of immense love that began to grow within me as all of my instincts and emotions were brought into play. Louise was beginning to touch every part of my being and it felt wonderful.

During her infancy she inspired a whole range of feelings within us. Frustration with her constant crying, anger at our loss of freedom, and, of course, the pure joy of touching, smelling and watching this wondrous thing grow. The tiny new teeth, the curly blonde hair, and those dark mysterious eyes that said so much and sometimes gave so much away. Almost with each new day she seemed to grow perceptibly. She displayed a vast range of emotions that she quickly learned to utilise to her advantage. She moved quickly between laughter and tears and like most infants she was hugely curious. She would beam and chatter incomprehensibly with each new discovery. In rapt concentration she examined that which to the adult eye warranted no more than a cursory glance. She became fascinated by birds, flowers, stones and cats. During the second year of her life cats took centre stage. As she grew she developed an overwhelming desire to place cats in containers, and would screech with delight to see a paw emerge from beneath its cardboard prison. Buckets, boxes or bags; it made no difference to Louise, they all became legitimate containers for cats.

Of course, these cats all belonged to other people, and eventually, or rather inevitably, she had to have one of her own. The first ones left home suffering from varying degrees of claustrophobia and with panic-stricken eyes. But finally Louise learnt that cats need freedom and persuaded one to stay with us permanently. This cat was, for many years, to become Louise's only friend.

We first noticed that things weren't quite as they should be by the number of times Louise would stumble and fall. She also began to become easily frustrated and annoyed when trying to write or draw. She was about three or four years old at the time and I clearly recall her biting pens and ripping paper in frustration. At the same time she would curse vociferously, but the tantrums didn't last long. In fact throughout her life she never lost her temper for long. She always hit the high spots quickly and, with equal speed, her anger always subsided.

The doctors couldn't, at first, understand what was going wrong. Perhaps she was just a clumsy child. After all we had enough torn tights and scuffed shoes to confirm that much. She always seemed to be falling over and having accidents. But why was she so clumsy and why did she hold her pencil in that awkward way? Her gait too was changing, she seemed to be developing a sort of limp, her left knee always slightly bent as she walked.

At four years of age Louise commenced her formal education. She made a disastrous start. She cried endlessly to come home, she refused to let go of the teacher's skirt, she was adamant that she would not go into the playground and decided, quite quickly, that other children were not half as interesting as cats, and most especially 'Benny' her imaginary best friend (also a cat).

By the time she was five Louise was living in a world of her own. Always reading and drawing. Engaging in long conversations with cats, both real and imaginary! She never brought a friend home nor even alluded to the existence of other children.

As time went by she became even more withdrawn. Her dark expressive eyes always half hidden behind a shock of tangled blonde hair. She seemed to prefer the company of adults and would dwell on their every word. Whenever we had friends round she would be found cross legged sitting nearby like some elfin creature from a fairy story. Not eager to please or intent upon showing off like so many five year olds, just listening, always listening and seemingly in deep thought.

She slept very little, preferring to read, draw or listen. She lived in a world of dreams, of wandering about the house and garden sometimes talking to herself and writing down stories about cats and her imaginary friend. In spite of her isolation at school she never seemed to be lonely. She developed an outrageous laugh that was to become something of her trademark in later life.

Her school reports said that she was inattentive, clumsy and not well socialised. Teachers perceived her as not being normal. They couldn't ever quite define what was happening, but I got the impression that they were not comfortable with Louise. With the benefit of hindsight I feel that the problem with my daughter was that teachers simply couldn't pigeon hole her. She was a 'one off' and did not conform to type.

As she approached junior school the reports worsened and her teachers became more menacing in their predictions for her future. The word 'maladjusted' (whatever that meant) was used to describe her demeanour and behaviour. All the while, at home, she continued to grow into a self-possessed and good natured, if somewhat eccentric, child. She was certainly a dreamer and those

9

dreams, for her, began to become reality as she withdrew further and further into her fantasy world. We explored her fantasies together, and began to write plays and stories about mythical creatures that inhabited a fantastic world. We acted out plays taking several different roles. In the morning she went to school exhausted from acting, drawing and writing.

For my part I was more than willing to indulge her, even though I sometimes found myself in embarrassing situations in public places as she would switch from being Louise (my young daughter) to some malevolent goblin that she had created the previous day. These switches would often occur at the most inopportune times. Once during school assembly she switched to goblin mode, climbed onto the stage and bit the head teacher on the ankle! We were, yet again, summoned into school to be told, in no uncertain terms that Louise's behaviour was symptomatic of some dark and menacing form of maladjustment, or worse. If all this had occurred say, in the late eighties, I am absolutely sure that we would, as parents, have been the subject of some investigations by over zealous social workers!

We were summoned into school time and again to be told that Louise wasn't socialised, that she was too withdrawn and that she dreamed too much – in short, her eccentricities were not acceptable. She saw bossy physiotherapists (for her limp) and they tried to bully her into walking in straight lines, she saw educational psychologists (for her eccentricities), and they told us that she wasn't happy. The head teacher, who had been bitten during assembly, told us that the best form of behaviour modification would be to sit Louise at the bottom of the stairs for long periods. We tried that – Louise was both mystified and amused by what she considered to be a rather boring and pointless game.

Finally, at the age of ten Louise saw a doctor at Booth Hall Children's Hospital in Manchester who diagnosed mild spastic diplegia. Her brain had been starved of oxygen during, or just after, her premature birth, her minor motor coordination (control of hands and feet) was consequently poor and she had developed an unusual gait as a coping strategy. As a result of her being different she had been rejected by her peer group in school and had become something of a figure of fun. She had created a happier world for herself elsewhere. Her poor performance in the classroom was caused, at least in part, by her feeling of being different because of her clumsiness and lack of dexterity and the resultant negative and sometimes aggressive response of those around her.

For many years Louise had suffered as result of a physical condition that she had had since birth. She had responded by creating and living in her own world and as a consequence had grown into an imaginative, articulate, strong willed and compassionate child who had learned to live without the approval of others. Her mild disability had played its part in the creation of an extraordinary character. She had, because she was different, developed the strength and determination to cope with the unimaginably more difficult challenge that was to confront her in the not too distant future.

By the time Louise was eleven she had been joined by two brothers and had displayed all the usual fascination, joy and petty jealousies that accompany such events. Although she had grown used to being the centre of attention she accepted Sam and then Barney with equanimity. Our close relationship remained unaltered. We had become comfortable living in the world that we created for ourselves. Sitting in the darkened corner of the garden on hot summer nights surrounded by the heady scent of night scented stocks, we talked of goblins under the bright stars until sleep gently claimed her. In the winter we wandered through the park on icy pink mornings feedings ducks or skimming broken chunks of ice across the deep frozen lake, Louise delighted in the whooping noises made by the spinning sparkling ice. On golden autumn afternoons we would walk through drifts of leaves talking and dreaming of the pixies and elves in the trees. At such times we found perfect peace together away from the rest of the world.

And so the bond between us grew ever stronger. Her knotted tangled hair was waist length and sun-streaked and she looked like a Pre-Raphaellite painting, with dark mysterious eyes softened through dreaming, and so expressive of all her innermost thoughts and feelings. Sometimes flashing in hot temper, sometimes tearful at some imagined slight or perceived injustice, but always so full of wonder, of questions and, of course, dreams.

By the time Louise had started at the local comprehensive she had developed enough verbal ability to defend herself against those from the other world, whose only form of pleasure seemed to come from humiliation they felt they could inflict upon those who were perceived to be different. Although undoubtedly sensitive to their taunts, she began to develop a tough exterior. She didn't feign indifference – she *was* indifferent.

Louise's life was not lived in school and her teachers quickly became aware of this. Her first school reports merely echoed those of her primary school. She is a dreamer, she is badly organised, she doesn't get on with the other pupils. Her isolation was exacerbated by the onset of puberty. Louise couldn't or wouldn't show any interest in boys, and clothes meant nothing to her other than as a necessity. She didn't wear make-up, but then she didn't need any. There was no make-up in the world that could have improved her perfectly clear olive skin. She shone with health and was as wild as nature.

During her first year at secondary school she was given endless detentions for not completing work or not being able to copy up notes on time. In spite of having received a detailed medical report indicating dyspraxia, the teachers did not seem either willing or able to accommodate her.

During one of these detentions she found herself alone with a boy two or three years her senior. Pascal Lam Bard was the school heartthrob and a boy with a nature as wild as Louise's. At the end of the detention, he turned, smiled at Louise, and without any warning set fire to the lines he had just completed. Louise was breathless with admiration having at last discovered a kindred spirit. Pascal Lam Bard was, tragically, to play a part in Louise's future.

Louise somehow never belonged to the town. She was a child of fields, woods and streams, and was happiest there, sitting with me for hour upon hour in shaded glades whilst I caught trout from some fast flowing stream or lake. On warm summer evenings we walked along riverbanks until my fishing became secondary to what was going on around us. Those halcyon days of her first year in secondary school were inevitably to end but our relationship remained strong and fulfilling and was to be tested to its limits before she had fully reached adulthood.

In the meantime Louise entered her second year at Collegiate High School and she began, at last, to take an interest in her studies. Encouraged by one or two perceptive teachers she began to grow in confidence. Her grades became markedly higher. Her interest in language, literature and music in particular seemed to develop almost overnight. She began to throw herself into her schoolwork. Puberty seemed to trigger not so much an interest in boys but a passion for study. She seemed desperate to learn, to develop her newly acquired skills. In that year she won the school prize for French and began to speak fluent German. Her confidence soared and she began to refer only fleetingly to her world of pixies and goblins.

At about this time Louise lost her beloved maternal grandfather. John Wilson was in his late sixties and although his death from a long-standing heart condition was not wholly unexpected, she was devastated. She wept bitterly for some time and then seemed to put her grief away, although it was obvious to us that she was grieving. She sensed that her grandmother Audrey (Nan) needed her to be strong. Nan was always especially close to Louise and had, over the years, become almost a second mother to her. Nan was to play an immensely important role in Louise's life during the next few years. Shortly after Grandpa's death Louise became a tower of strength. She spent hour upon hour with Nan, often packing her bags to spend a few nights with her. Louise loved to be needed and was always acutely aware of the pain that others were feeling. At this time Louise was very much needed and the bonding with Nan continued to develop as they became almost inseparable. I'm not sure how Louise ended up in the Tower Ballroom dancing with Nan – I had been commuting to Manchester to work each day and was seeing less of her than was customary. I do however, remember that enthusiasm for Blackpool Tower Ballroom didn't develop slowly. She quickly became obsessed with that huge baroque late Victorian ballroom and with everything connected with it. In short, the place had touched something deep within her.

She became like someone possessed. Every weekend, every day of every holiday she was there. She never did anything by halves. She learned to read music and spent hours, in spite of great difficulty with coordination, learning to play the organ – perhaps the most demanding of all instruments, requiring extremely well developed motor coordination in both hands and feet. It was almost as if she was determined to demonstrate, at least to herself, that she would not be limited in any way by anything so inconsequential as physical handicap.

During her thirteenth year she learned how to read and play music beautifully. Her confidence grew immeasurably, but still she found little or no pleasure in the company of other children. She never indulged in any of the early adolescent behaviour of her contemporaries. She found solace and gained great pleasure from playing and listening to music, visiting the Tower Ballroom with her Nan and, of course, sitting listening to adults sometimes until the early hours.

Even at thirteen she would occasionally approach me as I stood in the gathering darkness at the end of the garden after a hot summer's day. She would quietly ask me to talk about the goblins who lived in the huge sycamore tree next door, or of the elves who had taken up residence in the willow at the end of our garden. Of course I would willingly oblige for I enjoyed these moments at least as much as she did. And when I had finished my reverie she would smile knowingly and wrap her thin brown arms around my waist.

Similarly, she would never admit that Father Christmas didn't exist. Most children upon attaining the age of seven or eight would delight in telling their parents of their discovery of the truth. Louise always sought to perpetuate that which was magical, and yet in so many other ways her feet remained firmly on the ground.

Six months before Louise's fourteenth birthday we left our beloved house with its magical trees, goblins and elves. We left behind some very precious memories, and Louise seemed to leave behind her childhood. On the day we left she cried quietly as we said goodbye to our trees, to our special places and to our walks. As I watched her stoically gathering together her possessions I saw within her a strong independent young woman. There was no sentimentality in any of this. Louise was deeply moved by this leaving of her childhood. It was as if she knew that she had to move on and could never return to a place that had nurtured her so lovingly. I really cannot claim to know what lay behind those heartfelt tears but 'the heart has its reasons which reason knows nothing of' and Louise's heart seemed to have more reasons than most.

We moved to a middle-class suburb of Manchester so that I might be nearer to my work. It was comfortable, leafy and riddled with motorways. Louise seemed immediately to adjust to her new environment. It seemed as if she had just changed school uniforms and moved on. I am quite sure that this move was, for her, just as traumatic as it was other members of the family, but she showed little or no anguish or displeasure. She was, indeed, perhaps because of her unhappy experiences at school, becoming stoical. She had learned to put away some of her feelings. The dreaming child of nature was becoming a woman of the world.

Manchester was not an entirely happy experience. We had all the creature comforts of a good income and a beautiful house, but for some reason things just weren't the same as before. We had been happy in our semi with its beautiful garden full of trees. We didn't need two bathrooms with gold plated taps. Some people buy a house to show off, to try to prove something to others. Some people probably genuinely like having more space than they need. We loved atmosphere and the Manchester house just didn't have any.

Louise continued to develop her academic interests, adding Latin to her language interests. She continued to resist joining in with her contemporaries preferring her own company. Each morning I would walk her to school before going to work and each evening we walked and talked. But it was not the talk that we had enjoyed in the past. The humour was still there, in fact it had taken a marked turn towards satire, but the child had all but disappeared.

Every weekend she left home for her beloved Tower Ballroom, and every Sunday night we picked her up at the station to hear tales of the wonderful Wurlitzer organ. She longed to return to Blackpool and lived for those weekends with her Nan.

Shortly before her fifteenth birthday another influence entered

Louise life. She had by this time become completely fluent in German. She had commenced a correspondence with a German girl of her age and seemed to be gaining some satisfaction from this arrangement. Every so often a grey or pink envelope arrived bearing a German postmark. In response Louise would spend one or two evenings in her room replying to these letters. It became obvious to us that Karin was becoming the recipient of a lot of Louise's innermost thoughts and feelings. As far as she was concerned Karin was 'safe'. She knew nothing of Louise's mild handicap and so got to know the 'real' Louise. This friendship enabled Louise to spend a lot of time in Germany in years to come. She loved Germany and all things German.

Three weeks after Louise's fifteenth birthday we returned to live on the Fylde coast. We were all pleased to have arrived 'home' but Louise was especially happy. We enrolled her at the school she had left seventeen months before and set about renovating the very run down house that we had bought. It was a very happy time for us. It was a beautiful warm spring and I had resolved to spend more time at home. Moreover, we were out of the city and back to a semi-rural idyll away from traffic, crowds and the ever-present smell of exhaust fumes. I had taken a considerable drop in salary to make this move, but as I awoke on that first morning to the sound of birds instead of cars I knew that I had made the right decision. As usual Louise adjusted quickly to our move. The letters from Germany continued, as did her visits to the Tower, but still no friends visited. Louise seemed unconcerned, seemingly more than happy in the company of her Nan.

During the succeeding twelve months Louise studied hard for her GCSEs and made two visits to Germany. A boyfriend suddenly appeared and the bond between Louise and myself changed yet again. In so many ways she was growing ever more quickly away from her dependency upon me. I felt sad but also pleased for her. She was becoming very pretty with her beautiful tangled hair and dark eyes sometimes wistful and introspective but full of confidence now, and often poised on the edge of laughter.

School reports still touched on her eccentricities but the over-riding impression was of a young woman of tremendous academic potential with a growing self-belief. She often returned from school shaking with raucous laughter, having shared some boisterous or risqué joke with her taxi driver. Now banded in the more able sets and separated from the carnivores of her childhood, she began to make friends and gain considerable popularity in school. Each night she studied hard in her room and sometimes I would sit with her when she had finished and we would reminisce about times long past; of balmy summer evenings or snowy winter nights. But mostly we laughed. We began to share a sense of humour. Laughter and the need to laugh at oneself added a new dimension to the ways we built upon our love for one another. Laughter was to be an important ally in the battles we were to face together.

One hot morning in August 1987 my office telephone rang and her unmistakable voice was overflowing with excitement 'Daddy, I passed seven.'

She had also achieved some very high grades and had won the school modern language prize having achieved 'A' grades in both French and German. My mind flashed back to her childhood and all the gloomy predictions made with such certainty by her teachers. I felt hugely satisfied – we must have done something right after all!

Uncle Chris was delighted beyond measure. Chris Groves had been a friend since my schooldays. He was one of the brightest boys in his year but had left university before taking his finals. Nobody knows quite why he had done this, but most people were aware of his love of horse racing and night clubs. He was a highly intelligent, sensitive and somewhat eccentric individual, and had been devoted to Louise from the moment that she had uttered her first words and taken her first faltering steps. He had become Louise's champion during the darkest days of her childhood, and had convincingly dismissed her teachers as fools. He loved Louise and she reciprocated that love. Her examination results confirmed his faith in her and he predicted that she would enjoy a wonderful future – a future in which he was to play a vital role.

*

She spent two weeks in Germany during the summer of 1987 and

17

decided to study for 'A' levels at the local sixth form college. In the longer term she had decided to study German at university. During her two years in the sixth form Louise began to become much more outgoing, she gained a good deal of respect amongst her peers, many of whom began to turn to her for support or advice. They recognised that she had grown into a very independent young woman with a will of iron that often masked a very gentle heart.

As her 'A' level examinations approached Louise demonstrated a high level of self-discipline. She worked regularly and tirelessly. She never lost her sparkle or humour and always maintained a sense of proportion, recognising the need to enjoy herself and relax. She loved to have parties and drink Guinness. She seemed to get on well with most people but reserved her special affection for very few. On some occasions I could clearly see the child in her: she still dreamed, and every now and then her hot temper still flashed. At other times she seemed so strong, so independent and very self-willed. During these times she made me feel vulnerable and sometimes unsure of myself. I suppose I was, to some extent, afraid of losing her altogether as she grew to adulthood.

In the late summer of 1989 Louise reaped the rewards of two years' study. She gained the results she needed to secure her place at Leeds University to study on the German honours course. She also achieved the only 'A' grade 'A' level in German awarded at her sixth form college. We naturally felt very proud of her, but our pride and joy were tinged with the knowledge that in six weeks time she would be leaving us to start a new life of her own in Leeds. For her part Louise was overjoyed by the prospect of her independence. She was offered a place in the hall of residence of her choice and we began preparations for her imminent departure.

For the next three weeks Louise was ecstatically happy. She talked of her planned new life in Leeds with a mixture of excitement and trepidation. She went into town to buy clothes and all the bits and pieces that students living away from home cannot possibly survive without. During these weeks there was an aura of frenzied activity surrounding Louise.

Chapter Two

None of us will ever forget that morning in mid-September 1989. Louise had for some time been irritated by a small swelling on the instep of her right foot. She put this down to a new pair of shoes that she had bought a few weeks before and which had been poorly fitted. She had done nothing about this because the swelling was not causing any great inconvenience or pain. Her main purpose in making an appointment to see our GP that morning was to arrange to have this small irritant dealt with before she left for Leeds; after all she could ill afford to take time out from her precious studies.

Louise duly made her appointment and arranged for her mother to give her a lift to the surgery. I went into town to have my hair cut, and was mildly surprised when I returned home an hour or so later to find that they had not yet returned. Some time later Judy arrived home with Louise, they both looked tense and a little drawn. Louise was concerned that our GP had taken a blood sample and felt that he had seemed a little anxious, or at least she imagined that he had.

The following day we received a telephone call from the local cottage hospital requesting that Louise come to see the ortho-paedic surgeon the next day. This made me feel slightly uneasy. Things seemed to be moving just a little too quickly; after all we were only dealing with a small swelling on my daughter's instep, and it wasn't even painful. I felt that there was an unnecessary urgency about the whole situation. I began to suspect that things were not as they should be. The next day Judy drove Louise to see the consultant and I waited at home. They were a long time at the hospital and I reassured myself that there were probably many cases that day and that the consultant was running late.

Louise didn't just enter the house that day, she burst through the front door looking tearful, distressed and confused. Judy looked pale and worried, she told me that Louise was scheduled to have an operation to remove the swelling on the following afternoon. I tried to reassure her that this was normal procedure, given that she was due to start University early the following month. I told her that she was very lucky that they could fit her in at such short notice and that she would not have to bother with all this fuss when she got to Leeds, when after all, time would be so much more important. These assurances must have sounded hollow, for I did not believe a single word I was saying. My mouth was dry, my heart was racing and the biggest part of me was believing the worst.

The problem was she looked so well, so lovely on that bright late summer's day. Her waist length hair was streaked with blonde following a holiday in Spain. Her skin, newly tanned, glowed and radiated good health and her eyes sparkled. I began to notice the first signs of fear in her eyes but always tempered with determination. I had seen that look before and it gave me some strength, and better still, hope that things would be okay. That evening we sat together assuring one another that everything would be fine. By the end of the night Louise was laughing as she packed a bag to take to hospital the following day.

The next morning she was her usual bright, confident self. She was laughing and joking as she left the house bound for hospital and a minor surgical procedure. Judy drove her to the hospital as I had promised to look after a friend's child on that day. She was due to go into the operating theatre some time after lunch and was expected to be under anaesthetic for half an hour or so. As I tried to entertain my three-year-old charge my thoughts constantly slipped away to the wonderful days of Louise's childhood, a world to which on that fateful day, I was eager to return.

Judy returned home as Louise was wheeled into theatre, and we sat back to await a call from the hospital saying everything had gone well. Some two hours later the phone had still refused to ring, the silence became palpable and the looks exchanged between us became increasingly fearful. Our friend arrived to collect his child and, naturally, assured us that there wouldn't be a problem. After all, it was only a minor operation. We telephoned a few friends and, of course, everybody knew of some perfectly legitimate reason as to why such a routine procedure should have taken over two hours. Finally, not convinced by numerous well meant but nonetheless unconvincing explanations, Judy plucked up the courage to phone the hospital. She looked very frightened as she came into the living room. She was told that Louise was still in theatre, but that there was nothing to worry about. Another hour went by and Judy was becoming increasingly tearful. Two more calls and two more standard reassurances later and we were in the car and heading for South Shore hospital to find out what was happening to our daughter.

It was about 6 p.m. when we arrived there on that dull cold September evening. Louise had been in theatre for about four hours and we were almost at breaking point. As we entered the dark portals of the old building we were met by the sister in charge who, in a matter-of-fact, almost flippant manner, asked who we had come to visit. We introduced ourselves and her manner changed abruptly. The three of us seemed to freeze at the same time. There was an awkward silence which seemed to last an age, until I heard myself sounding panic stricken and demanding to know where my daughter was. The nurse, sounding far from reassuring, countered with the least reassuring response imaginable, 'Would you like to go into the office for a cup of tea?'

I remember making some vaguely rude remark about cups of tea and sitting down in a dimly lit office that had not been decorated in living memory. The nurse disappeared and we sat in silence fully expecting to be told that Louise had died in theatre. As it transpired we were not far wrong.

The kindly, but distinctly uncomfortable, Asian doctor explained in a faltering voice that the consultant had successfully removed the growth from Louise's instep and had sent a sample of tissue away for tests. I asked him why the operation had taken so long and he became evasive and uneasy. I was having some difficulty understanding his heavy accent and I became impatient and angry. He seemed to be waiting for the arrival of a more senior doctor and was successfully evading my direct questioning. I managed to ascertain that the recently removed growth did not look benign, but was then promptly assured that looks were very often deceptive. The conversation began to go around in circles as he became more and more discomfited by my growing irritation at his evasiveness. I cannot remember much about the content of that conversation, but I can remember clearly something that we were going to see a great deal of in the eyes of health professionals during succeeding months – this doctor's eyes were full of fear and pity.

After twenty minutes or so this poor doctor was put out of his misery by the arrival of Louise's anaesthetist. He explained clearly, and with some authority, that upon removing the growth from her foot, the consultant surgeon had administered a precautionary injection of vincristine, an anti-cancer drug. Louise had responded by going into bronchial arrest, ceasing to breathe and, because of this potential fatal reaction, she was to be transferred that evening to the intensive care unit of our main hospital in Blackpool for observation. The operation had taken so long because the growth had been found to extend deep within the healthy tissue of Louise's right foot. We were devastated – anti-cancer drugs, intensive care, bronchial arrest. This quite simply wasn't the language associated with minor routine surgery on a healthy eighteen-year-old. The anaesthetist asked if we would like to see Louise in the recovery room prior to her transfer; I declined whilst Judy agreed. I just couldn't face seeing her at that terrible moment, and to this day I still don't know why. I did, however, edge closer to the recovery room. Just close enough to see her pale thin hand punctured by multicoloured tubes and seemingly held together with elastoplast, clutching a well worn grubby orange teddy bear that we had bought for her when she was two years old. As I walked towards the car on the chill September night I started to cry the first of many tears.

The following morning we visited her in intensive care. The unit was full of people whose tenuous hold on life was seemingly dependent upon remaining connected to numerous machines which whirred, bleeped and hummed reassuringly. As I looked for Louise I reflected on the ephemeral nature of existence, fully expecting to find her similarly wired to life guarded by a machine. We found her in a little side bay and immediately I saw her my worst fears were allayed. She looked perfectly healthy sitting up in bed eating a yoghurt. The sun was streaming into the room and it seemed for a brief moment that the events of the previous night had been a terrible nightmare.

Louise began to describe 'the wonderful experience' that she had had during her transfer between hospitals. She had not stopped breathing just once during her operation, but had suffered another bronchial arrest in the ambulance whilst being transported to intensive care. She described, in great detail, how she had 'died' during the journey and found it to be a wonderful and almost blissful experience. She described how she had drifted 'out of her body' towards a beautiful light. This light emanated a great peace and was perceived by Louise to be the embodiment of goodness. All the while beneath her she was observing the doctors and ambulance crew desperately trying to get her breathing again. She explained that she did not wish to return to her body but wanted to continue drifting towards this 'light'. She seemed disappointed when she found herself back in the ambulance feeling the pain from her right foot. She was laughing and joking and it became clear to us that the doctors hadn't told her about her injection of vincristine. Louise simply assumed that she had reacted badly to the anaesthetic. Judy was concerned that Louise might have suffered some form of brain damage during the time that she had stopped breathing, she asked her to recite the long telephone number of her German penfriend and was greatly relieved to find that she could recall it. I glanced at her right foot, now encased in plaster from knee to toe. I shuddered to think just what that innocuous looking plaster cast might contain.

The following day the doctors moved her to a main ward where she was given a comfortable side room. Her tissue sample was sent for examination and she was as bright and bubbly as ever. I began to assure myself that even if the tests showed that she did indeed have cancer, it was in her right foot, as far away from vital organs as it was possible to get. I thought that even if she had to have her foot amputated then at least she would be alive and anyway she would adapt just as she always had done. I became comfortable with these thoughts. People around us were, as ever, expressing equally optimistic sentiments. Louise's hospital room overflowed with flowers and cards, and she began to enjoy all the attention. My mind began to shut out the reality of just why she was in hospital as I concentrated on making her happy. But all the time I knew that one day soon the dreaded test results would arrive at the hospital and I prayed that they would not show any malignancy.

I shall never forget that Friday evening. She had been in hospital for two days and, comforted by our optimism and the support of friends we had begun to actually feel quite hopeful that all would be well. We enjoyed the bright atmosphere of her room and even the routine of visiting, meeting friends there, taking treats for Louise and listening to her outrageous laughter which greeted us as we walked down the long corridor on our frequent daily visits. I remember that it was about 6 p.m., or perhaps slightly later, as we approached Louise's ward. Everything seemed strangely silent. The nurses who would normally be busy cheerfully ministering to their patients were huddled around the desk in the middle of the ward. The curtains were pulled closed on the window of Louise's room and as we approached I sensed that something was horribly wrong.

As we entered her dimly lit room. I could hear her softly crying. She was holding Nan's hand. Nan was obviously in some distress and seemed to be having great difficulty holding back her own tears. Louise slowly turned her tear streaked face towards me.

'I've got cancer, Daddy,' she almost spat out, and then began to sob loudly, 'I'm probably going to die.'

Her consultant had visited her with the results of her tests a little while earlier. He had waited for our arrival, but could wait no longer. He had, quite rightly, told Louise that her tissue sample was malignant because she had asked for the truth. She was, after all, eighteen years old, and had a right to be treated as an adult.

I felt an almost uncontrollable anger. I wanted to blame someone, I needed a target. I quietly cursed him for telling her. Why couldn't he tell me so I could soften the blow for her? I should have told her – who does he think he is? I left Louise's room and looked up and down the ward in case he hadn't left. I needed a victim for my anger, anguish and shock. I looked helplessly at the group of nurses and they returned my look as if to say 'how is he going to cope with this'. It was the same look of fear and pity that I had received from that Asian doctor following Louise's operation.

One by one the nurses melted away into side wards. They didn't know what to say. What solace could they offer in this awful situation. I felt numb, angry, alone and useless. I couldn't face Louise, I couldn't bear her emotional pain. What could I offer her now? I felt like running away to find somewhere quiet where I could gather my senses.

I was seriously contemplating doing precisely that when a nurse in a different uniform emerged from Louise's room. I hadn't been aware of her presence when I had first entered the room some minutes earlier. She placed her hand on my arm and began to speak quietly. I repaid her kindness with anger. I began to ramble. I told her to go away and leave me alone. She took a step back, all the time maintaining eye contact. I sensed that she knew just how much pain I was suffering. She wasn't frightened by my anger, nor did she encourage it. She just waited, she knew what was coming next. My heart burst and the tears flowed. I don't remember how long I cried, but she must have sensed an end to it because she stepped towards me, placed her hand on my arm and looked into my bloodshot eyes.

'One day at a time, Philip,' she said quietly, 'you must now begin to live your life just one day at a time.'

She spoke of Louise's love for me and of her great need of my support. She knew exactly what to say, she made me feel needed. She talked of the nature of cancer and of the role I would have to play in caring for Louise. She made me feel more positive, but most important of all, when I looked into her eyes she showed neither pity or fear.

She was the first person I was to meet who worked every day with cancer. I was, of course, to meet many more and they were all recognisable, as was that Macmillan nurse, by their under-standing, their commitment and their complete lack of fear. Other health professionals are no doubt dedicated and compassionate, but I was to discover that this particular disease requires a different approach when dealing with both victims and their families. Those who did not specialise in this area of medicine were always to display at least a modicum of discomfort in our presence. I can't remember just how long I spent on that corridor but I do remember feeling very different from the man who had rushed out of that room in panic and anger some time earlier. I felt much more calm, and by now so did Louise. Her face was flushed and pink and her eyes were red, but she smiled from behind the last of her tears. She told me with genuine conviction that we were not going to lose and that she would live.

The following morning we were due to meet Louise's consultant surgeon. I remember that it was a bright and warm autumnal morning. In spite of the events of the previous evening I was feeling optimistic as we approached Louise's ward for our meeting. We were directed to a small office and, of course, offered a cup of tea. A few minutes later Mr Boardman entered and introduced himself. I noticed that he seemed very uncomfortable and that his eyes seemed to be full of tears. He measured his words carefully as he spoke but sometimes his voice faltered. He seemed to be a very gentle and sensitive man and it was obvious that he was having great difficulty conducting this interview. He told us that an examination of Louise's tumour had shown that it was malignant. He went on to explain that a more detailed examination would be carried out at Christie Hospital in Manchester to determine the type of cancer from which Louise was suffering. He carefully explained that some types of cancer were more easily treatable than others, and that in about a week's time we would know a great deal more about the particular nature of Louise's cancer. I asked him if Louise was going to die, and he told me that all cancers were life threatening. I left the meeting knowing little more than I had known the previous evening, but I contented myself with the thought that Louise may well have an eminently treatable type of cancer. I kept reminding myself of the words of that Macmillan nurse: 'one day at a time, Philip, one day at a time'. These words were to prove invaluable during future crises.

We joined Louise in her bright flower bedecked room. By now word had got out that she had cancer. Ahead of us lay the terrible task of telling friends and relatives. For the time being, though, the three of us sat together as the soft autumn sunshine slanted through her window, glancing off the untouched bowls of fruit and bottles of cordial. We sat together trying calmly to assess the situation, and time and again came to the same conclusion. The cancer was in her foot, not her liver or any other vital organ. It was most probably the easiest type to treat, and all this would soon be behind us. Forgetting the maxim 'one day at a time' we rushed forward into a future where everything would be all right. We left the hospital that morning to disseminate the truth, as far as we understood it, to friends and relatives. We were simply not prepared for the response.

There followed one of the most hectic weeks of our lives. Once the phone calls had been made the invasion began. We arrived at Louise's room the next day to find that a queue had formed outside her door. Inside, Louise was happily holding court, lying on her bed with her right leg stiffly extended in plaster. People around her appeared as acolytes hanging on to her every word. She was by now special, all the more so because she had cancer and appeared to be making light of it. In truth, she was really very frightened inside but was not really being given the chance to sit back and properly assess this dreadful situation. Conversations were all about 'now', nobody ventured to talk about what the future might hold for her. Of course, everybody knew somebody who had survived this disease, sometimes against the most daunting odds. That first week following diagnosis of malignancy became something of a circus. Louise didn't have time to think, but maybe that was just as well.

About a week later she was moved to Christie Hospital for further tests and at this point she began to show some fear, even a little panic. She had moved from that which was familiar and safe to a place which was, at that time, unknown, and for her, full of the most awful connotations of sickness and death. She was placed in the Children's Unit even though she was eighteen. This was a very positive move. This unit, unlike the adult wards, was brightly decorated, sunny and above all optimistic in its outlook. Not only that, it was full of children and young people who were suffering in the same way as Louise, and I am sure that to some extent she was consoled by this.

Louise spent the next few days in Christie undergoing detailed tests. In spite of visiting, we missed her awfully. Then one evening the telephone rang. It was a cousin of Judy's who happened to be in Manchester on business. He had called in to see

Louise and to her great joy the doctors decided that she could come home for a few days. He drove Louise home to us and as she walked, supported by her zimmer frame into the light of the hall I could see just how the time at Christie had affected her. She looked very tired and tense. She was breathing very heavily as she struggled pitifully with her frame. Her eyes were full of frustration and despair and she seemed close to tears. She needed to use the toilet and she had to heave herself upstairs on her bottom dragging her plaster clad right leg behind her. She refused all offers of help and as we stood meekly by I could sense the outburst coming.

'I've had enough of all this – why me, why did it have to happen to me?'

She started to cry and shout. As I watched her sitting half way up the darkened stairs sobbing I felt utterly useless. She had spent three days being prodded, poked and stuck full of needles. She had been surrounded by children undergoing chemotherapy. She understood nothing of what was going on around her. All she knew was that she too, at some point, was going to lose her lovely hair and spend days on end vomiting whilst turning pale grey just like all the others. That night she had arrived home for a short respite from all of that horror, and home had suddenly reminded her of all she had lost. We let her cry until finally, as always, she managed to see an amusing side to the situation.

'Oh, my God, Daddy, it's pathetic. I'm eighteen years old, I'm stuck in a zimmer frame and the only way I can get upstairs is by shuffling on my fucking arse!'

She started to laugh, and at that moment I felt tears begin to prick my eyes. If she can laugh at this I thought, she could laugh at anything. She was indeed special.

Louise was moved back to her room at Christie after a precious, and sometimes difficult weekend at home. Nan travelled back with her, or at least visited her the following day, I cannot fully remember. In any case she telephoned us on her return to Blackpool: 'Dr Rao needs to speak to you both urgently on Wednesday.'

We became very frightened, this was something we had tried to put out of our minds. Wednesday was tomorrow and I wished she had said Thursday or better still Friday. I had been living one day at a time and the next day was to be the most important of our lives.

It was late October 1989 and as we drove down the motorway on that warm autumn morning I felt a great foreboding. We didn't speak during that one hour journey, I just remember a lot of roadwork cones flashing past the car window. My thoughts were of autumns long past when, with her small hand clutching mine, we would go to feed the ducks in the park kicking leaves at one another as she screeched with delight. This day was very different and as we pulled up in the car park, I felt the icy hand of the inevitable clutch at my heart. As we walked towards the Children's Unit I remember praying that this was just a nightmare; that I would wake up to find her lying beside me surrounded by crayons and freshly drawn pictures of goblins! Once inside we walked straight to Louise's room and I dreaded the sound of some nurse's voice calling to us, 'Dr Rao will see you now, Mr and Mrs Woolcock.'

I didn't want to see Dr Rao now, or at any other time. In fact, I remember wishing that he had gone home sick, or better still died.

Louise was sitting on her bed complaining that she was bored. She wanted to come home again. Conversation was difficult. We were preoccupied by our imminent meeting and Louise with her boredom and the fact that her newly bandaged foot was itching. Every now and again I observed that a small dark Asian man in a white coat was pacing up and down the corridor outside. He looked preoccupied and a little tense. I had not yet met Dr Rao, the consultant oncologist in the Children's Unit, and I hoped that this man wasn't him because he looked as if he was preparing to give somebody some bad news. The man disappeared up the corridor and a few minutes later Jane (Louise's nurse) came into the room to summon us to Dr Rao's office. We lifted Louise into her wheelchair and wheeled her to meet her fate.

Dr Rao, a Sri Lankan with a gentle self-effacing manner, sat calmly at his desk. He was indeed that man who I had seen nervously pacing the corridor not five minutes before. He welcomed us and beckoned for us to sit opposite him. Louise was wheeled round to sit alongside Judy and Jane sat beside Louise. It was a small room and I began to wonder about the yellow box of Kleenex tissues on his desk, perhaps he was suffering from a cold. Behind him were pictures of what I took to be X-rays of Louise, or at least parts of her, whilst in front on his desk was a bulky file with Louise's name clearly printed on the spine.

There was a few seconds awkward silence before Louise addressed Dr Rao in a 'well, out with it man' sort of way. Dr Rao seemed glad of Louise's timely intervention and proceeded to explain carefully and quietly that upon further examination he had discovered that her cancer was not confined to her right instep. Cancer cells had been found in her right knee, her shoulder and her spine. He described these cells as 'traces'. Louise asked nervously if she would have to have her leg amputated (this had by now become her greatest fear), and was relieved when Dr Rao made it clear that this would not constitute a part of her treatment. He went on to explain that Louise would have to undergo a programme of chemotherapy and some radiotherapy treatment and that this programme was harsh and would last for up to eighteen months. He spoke of the nature of chemotherapy and of the horrendous side effects. We had difficulty taking much of this information in. Dr Rao realised this and suggested that Jane take Louise back to her room to talk in more detail about his proposed course of treatment and to answer any questions that she might have. I was relieved, thinking that we were leaving too. I didn't want to hear any more, I just wanted to get out of that small room. My feeling at that time was that Dr Rao had found a cure for her, and in spite of some side effects, she was going to get better.

I made to move from my chair but Dr Rao indicated that he would like us both to stay. Louise looked apprehensive as Jane wheeled her out of the room. Dr Rao told her that he needed to speak to Mum and Dad about the side effects of the treatment and that he wouldn't keep us for much longer. Jane reappeared having left Louise in her room. Dr Rao's demeanour changed and he became very serious. Jane was looking very concerned and had moved to sit closer to Judy. Dr Rao explained that Louise was suffering from rhabdomyosarcoma, a vicious cancer which affects muscle tissue and is found usually in children. I asked him what chance of survival Louise had, and he said less than ten per cent. I refused to hear him and replied that fifty per cent offered us some hope. I have no idea as to why I decided arbitrarily that she had a fifty per cent chance. I suppose that my mind just couldn't accept his figure and so offered one of its own. Dr Rao didn't pull his punches, he confirmed his grim prognosis by stating unequivocally that rhabdomyosarcoma, at this stage, was almost always fatal, that it was likely that in spite of treatment Louise would die.

I can remember him coming quickly round the desk and putting his arm around my shoulder; I can remember him reaching for the box of Kleenex tissues and the look of sheer pity on Jane's face. She had no words of comfort, and although she had witnessed this scene a hundred or more times I could tell that she still felt the same pain each time. I remember feeling a huge emotional pain well up from somewhere deep in the centre of my being followed by deep sobbing and burning tears. I can't remember just how long I cried, but when I had finished I looked at Judy who stared horror struck at nowhere in particular. She seemed to be desperately trying to focus on the awfulness of this situation. She seemed unable to cry or show any other emotion, she just sat there stunned, all her senses frozen in terrible disbelief.

Although in intense shock we managed to ask some questions, and naturally we wanted to know just how long our precious daughter had to live. Dr Rao explained that he had devised a radical treatment programme for Louise that would mean that she would have to attend Christie for about eighteen months to undergo chemotherapy and radiotherapy. He was going to attack her cancer in spite of the odds. He was going to subject her body to a regime of extremely toxic chemicals. He explained to us that Louise would become awfully debilitated, that she would suffer violent nausea and that she would lose all of her beautiful hair. He proffered a chart upon which he had outlined a pattern of treatment. For the first three months she would have to spend one week in two at Christie being bombarded with chemicals and X-rays. She would return home for the second week to enable partial recovery and then in this debilitated state she would once again

31

embark upon what she came to call her week of hell. Dr Rao explained the many problems associated with such treatment. He laid great emphasis on the fact that Louise would become very prone to infection and that this might sometimes be life threatening as the toxins broke down and then annihilated her immune system. At the end of three months her programme would become less severe, in that she would spend two weeks at home for every week of treatment.

We left Dr Rao's office that terrible day having absorbed only a fraction of what he had told us. I can remember being particularly upset at the fact that she was going to lose her hair. This may seem illogical, but I don't think that there can be a 'normal' reaction to being told effectively that your child is going to die, but until that happens she will be subjected to a long period of pain and nausea.

As I walked towards Louise's room I was trying to control another tide of tears that had begun to well up inside me. I tried desperately to compose myself. Louise mustn't suspect that I am upset – 'one day at a time, Philip, one day at a time'. I kept repeating the words of the Macmillan nurse over and over. At least Louise is alive today. She is not going to die today; tomorrow doesn't matter. With these thoughts racing through my mind I walked a couple of circuits of the children's ward all the time putting off going to see her.

When I finally made it to Louise's room, she was lying on her bed talking to Jane who was gently explaining to her the problems with, and nature of, her proposed programme of treatment. She smiled as I walked in. She looked a little worried, but there was determination behind her smile. It was a smile that I was to see so often in the future. She asked me if I was okay. This was typical of her. Throughout her illness she was to show great concern for others, she never made people feel uncomfortable about being around her. She didn't let her cancer spoil things for other people, there was never any self pity in her. I found this remarkable in one so young and so desperately ill. I sat down on Louise's bed and told her everything was going to be fine and that we would beat this thing together. She gave me a hug and then proudly produced her treatment chart. She was extremely concerned about losing her hair, but equally relieved that she was not going to lose her leg. I secretly wished that amputation had been an option, for that would have meant that her cancer had not spread into the rest of her body and she would have had a fighting chance. As it was she was very probably going to die and there was, in my view, no way of telling an eighteen-year-old young woman this awful prognosis because she may simply have stopped fighting. I believe to this day that it was right to lie to her.

We left Louise that day to her doctors, they had further tests to carry out. More blood samples, more needles, more poking and prodding. She hated all that but she remained stoical as she prepared herself for the battle for her life. She waved us away with an uncertain smile and I remember vividly her hair catching the pale autumn sun as it danced through her window. A part of me was trying hard to accept that I was going to lose her, but I could never bring myself to believe it. It was just too horrible to contemplate and so I thought about today. Today she was alive and that was all that mattered. Tomorrow may never come. I was conscious that I had begun, at last, to live for one day at a time.

We drove back up the motorway in almost total silence, our senses in shock, our emotions in a spin, not able to make sense of anything, they had just shut down. That evening I watched a boxing match on TV but I can't remember who won.

The next day I awoke with a jolt of horror. For a few seconds I thought that I must have dreamt it all. I lay staring at the ceiling for a while, while the emotional pain came flowing back to flood my senses. We had to telephone friends and relations, and I wasn't sure how we were going to go about this. I cannot remember making the difficult telephone calls but I vaguely remember people's reactions to the dreadful news. The sanctimonious became pious and those who felt the least moved pronounced the greatest love for her. Uncle Chris was simply devastated, and, for a time, seemed to go into denial.

Louise's treatment was scheduled to start in a few days time and none of us knew just what to expect. How on earth are they going to transform a seemingly healthy young woman into somebody who looks like they have just been liberated from a concentration camp. I had seen the children at Christie, but couldn't for the life of me imagine that Louise could ever look like them. I was, of course, wrong.

Chapter Three

During Louise's childhood I had got to know our GP quite well. Over a number of years we had become friends, but when we moved to Manchester we lost touch and had not seen one another for five or six years. He had also become quite close to Louise and they had often gone for long walks together on the beach with his dogs. David Cooper was very much in my thoughts on the day we visited Christie to receive that terrible diagnosis.

Most notably, David had been the driving force behind the building of a new hospice on the Fylde coast. I can remember his enthusiasm for this project and my total lack of interest at the time. For some reason he had been keen for me to understand the nature of hospices. He had even driven me to Manchester, during the building of the Blackpool hospice, to visit St Ann's Hospice so that I could see for myself what wonderful places they were. I remember being distinctly unimpressed, reasoning that those with terminal illness should simply get on with dying. Arguing that valuable resources should be targeted at those with some hope of recovery. In the coming months I was to dramatically change my views.

The morning after Louise's diagnosis I was staring out of the kitchen window trying to marshal my thoughts into a semblance of order, the doorbell rang and a concerned looking David Cooper announced that he had received a call from Dr Rao at Christie Hospital the previous day. It occurred to me that at some time during my conversation with Dr Rao I must have talked about David. It transpired that when asked if there was anybody that I wanted to speak to I had, in my painful confusion, given David's name.

We sat in the living room and he listened as we tried, with difficulty, to express our feelings of devastation and our fear of, what to us, was the unknown. We simply didn't have any understanding of just what we had to face. As Medical Director at

Trinity Hospice, David Cooper was ideally placed to explain in detail the nature of the care and support that Louise would need during her treatment. As our understanding developed so our fears diminished. We began to steel ourselves for the long battle ahead. It was going to be murderously tough, but we were not going to be found wanting. At that time we had no idea of just how much we were to achieve in the future, our only concern was to make Louise as happy and comfortable as possible.

Louise's chemotherapy was to be administered via a tube directly into her bloodstream. The week before her treatment began she had undergone a minor operation to have a small device fitted just beneath her collar bone. At the start of each treatment Louise would have a tube attached to this device through which the toxic chemicals would be pumped into her. This cocktail of deadly chemicals would attack and destroy her cancer cells, but they were not selective in that they also destroyed healthy cells, most notably, hair and stomach cells. Violent nausea and hair loss are the notorious trademark of chemotherapy.

On the first day of treatment we arrived at Christie to find Louise sitting up in bed as Jane attached her to toxic drips. Jane flicked a switch and a clear orange coloured liquid moved menacingly along the clear tube and into Louise's body. Louise began calmly to read a book. We waited in anticipation to see what would happen. We just didn't know what to expect. We certainly didn't expect Louise to announce brightly that she fancied a large hamburger and fries from Macdonalds. When this request came I was completely taken aback and absolutely delighted. Perhaps Louise was not going to suffer horrendous side effects after all. Eager to oblige and in the vain hope that Louise was going to confound all medical opinion we drove a couple of miles and brought her a large portion of fast food which she proceeded to consume enthusiastically. I watched in awe and wonder as each mouthful disappeared. She passed me the empty polystyrene container, and as she did she started to change colour. It was to be the first of many bouts of violent nausea, and as I watched I shook with trepidation for the power of that retching and heaving was awesome. I learned in that moment that the nausea of chemotherapy is nothing like that associated with, say, a stomach upset.

Her whole body seemed to be in spasm, every part of her shook as she vomited. The poison had taken hold, it was killing cancer cells already, but how much of my daughter would it kill. As she wiped away the tears of exertion she smiled and then she cursed. I picked up the book that she had been reading and noticed that my hand was trembling.

She soon became drowsy from the exertion of constant nausea and we decided to travel home whilst she slept. As we drove home north, Nan drove south to be with Louise. Her support for her beloved granddaughter was priceless during the whole of Louise's illness. We had her two young brothers to care for and could not spend all our time at Christie whilst Louise underwent her torture. Nan sat with her day and night, even though for most of the time Louise was either asleep or at best very drowsy.

After four and a half days treatment Nan brought her home. She looked very pale and there were dark bags beneath her eyes, but she was smiling. Best of all she still had her beautiful hair, although much shorter now. We had asked a hairdresser to cut it down to about two inches in preparation for the inevitable. She limped along the hallway supported by that despised zimmer frame. She was so pleased to be back home even though it would only be for a week. She was too weak and tired to stay downstairs with us for long and retired to her bedroom soon after her arrival home. That bedroom was to become her special place in the months to come. She found great comfort there amongst her souvenirs, trophies and books. Her room was an extension of her personality; full of bright colours and music. It became a retreat from the harshness of reality, but more importantly it was something that belonged to her, a private haven of peace and tranquillity far away from Christie hospital.

About fifteen minutes had passed when I heard that chilling sound of violent retching. Again and again she strained as her body reacted to four days of invasion by toxic chemicals. Downstairs I quietly prayed that each heave and cry would be the last. With each spasm my anger grew. My own stomach tightened and my fists clenched. There was nothing I could do. I had allowed the doctors to literally poison her and this was the result of their efforts. A part of me hated them for what they had done to her.

Just as I felt my anger and despair reach a crescendo the retching stopped; everything went eerily silent and I went upstairs not knowing what to expect. Louise was sitting on the bed holding an NHS issue grey cardboard sick bowl which was filled with bile-soiled tissues. I sat beside her and put my arm around her thin shoulder. She was trembling even though the room was warm. She squeezed my hand and tried to smile behind her tears. She was gasping for breath.

'Are you all right, Daddy?' she said.

Am I all right? What sort of a question was that? She always asked the same thing whenever I looked even mildly distressed. The more ill she became the more she seemed concerned for those around her. I was to learn that many children who suffer the ravages of cancer behave in this selfless way.

'I'm hungry now,' she said and my heart leapt for joy.

I desperately wanted to nurture her. I needed to be needed, and right now I felt indispensable. At this point we began to establish the beginning of what was to become an important routine. Judy did the run to Christie and I looked after the boys and made sure that everything was ready on those wonderful days when she arrived home after her treatment. She ate a chopped egg that day and kept it down. I was delighted.

A day or two later as I sat in her room I noticed in horror that the parting in her hair had grown noticeably wider and that there were small tufts of golden hair on her pillow. Louise too was aware of this sinister development and looked at me fearfully. I picked up the hairbrush and gently stroked it through her hair. It came out by the handful, balls of gold leaving large bald patches all around her head. Judy arrived with my beard trimmer and began to shave off the few remaining strands. The chemotherapy had done its work and Louise was completely bald. She cried, then laughed, then cursed in anger at this long-dreaded development. But by the end of the week she looked quite fashionable and began to compensate for the loss of her hair by wearing bright makeup, garish nail varnish and outrageous earrings.

The day before she lost her hair Louise had attended a press conference. For some time, shortly after her diagnosis, we had been toying with the idea of using her terrible situation to, in some way, raise awareness, or even funds for others in a similar situation. We had settled on the idea of helping David Cooper to build a much needed day hospice as an extension to the established Trinity Hospice. Whilst David was sympathetic to our aims, he doubted that we would have the energy, or even necessary skills to undertake this adventure. He advised us to concentrate upon dealing with Louise's cancer and treatment. We disagreed and 'The Louise Woolcock Cancer Support Fund' was launched and registered as a charity at the end of October 1989. The press launch was an immediate success and offers of help and support came flooding in. By the end of November we had raised more than twenty thousand pounds. This charity was to lead us into adventures of which we could only have dreamed.

Meanwhile, we began to establish our routine of one week's treatment followed by a week at home to enable Louise to make a partial recovery before her return for another week's torture. Her chemotherapy regime was unimaginably harsh and its physical effects upon her were devastating and unremitting. She became very pale and weak and lost a lot of weight. The rings fell from her fingers and her eyebrows and eyelashes disappeared. Even worse, though, were the infections. They swept through her like a forest fire. Typically, she complained of a severe headache. This was quickly followed by intense shivering and other flu-like symptoms.

I particularly remember one wet cold November night when she began to suffer the onset of an infection. It was late, about midnight, and we simply could not face the drive to Christie. We were exhausted and decided, instead, to call our GP. I remember a young locum arriving at the front door looking distinctly nervous. I described Louise's condition and her symptoms. He looked very worried as he examined her. She cried out in pain and delirium. He had probably never treated a young cancer patient before and he decided to administer an intravenous shot of valium to help her sleep. He left with instructions to call him in the morning should her condition worsen. Louise went into a deep sleep whilst her infection spread quickly through her emaciated body. With no real immune system in place she didn't stand a chance of making any sort of recovery. She very nearly died. The following morning she was rushed by ambulance to Christie and put on an antibiotic drip. We had, through sheer exhaustion, disobeyed one of the cardinal rules. Whenever she became ill in the future we took her down the motorway, whatever the circumstances, to the people who knew about cancer. However well meaning doctors were, it seemed to us that they were out of their depth when dealing with this very special disease.

As our routines and systems became established so it became easier for us to cope with whatever the cancer would throw at us. By Christmas 1989 we had completed a very steep learning curve and seemed prepared for any eventuality. We were emotionally shattered but our commitment to Louise and her illness remained total. The support that we were receiving from Christie was phenomenal. Nothing was too much trouble; everything was explained to us in fine detail. The nursing staff were tremendous, they went to great lengths to allay our fears and were utterly dedicated to Louise's care. A social worker was appointed to help us deal with Louise and to enable us to come to terms with our situation. Wendy Murphy was to become a friend, confidante and ally to all of us.

Our first Christmas with cancer will live with us for ever. Just three months into our 'new life' and we were about to turn a very important corner. Louise's chemotherapy regime was to become a little less demanding. From January she would spend two weeks at home for every five days treatment at Christie. This meant that her body would have more time to recover between treatments, and thus she would become a little stronger and more mobile. I was quietly contemplating the positive implications of all of this as I was hanging the two hundred and fifteenth Christmas card when Louise came through the front door grumbling and cursing. She was attempting to drag behind her a huge sack of presents that had been provided by Christie. She would accept no help, and was becoming increasingly angry and frustrated by her inability to move her Christmas presents more than a few feet down the hallway. As her language became stronger I was reminded of those temper tantrums years before caused by her lack of dexterity. She hadn't changed at all.

She looked utterly drained and very thin, and I remember

thanking God that her regime was going to become a little easier. I don't thing that she could have survived for much longer on her week in week out programme. As she came into the living room she smiled weakly, 'Sorry about the language, Daddy.'

She was so happy to be at home. She slumped into her chair and I noticed just how much this latest treatment had taken out of her. Her eyes were dull, the sparkle had all but gone, she was waxen pale and had lost perhaps two stones in weight in just three months. But she was looking forward to two whole weeks at home where she would grow marginally stronger. I went into the kitchen to cook for her and when I returned she had fallen into a deep sleep exactly where I had left her. She looked not unlike a refugee from a concentration camp, and yet she was still beautiful. Her spirit remained untouched by all the horrors to which she had been subjected.

I had, by this time, all but given up work to look after her and to spend as much time with her as I could. The charity gained momentum and Louise was rapidly becoming something of a celebrity. We began to get to know one another as we had when she was a child, and I loved having her back. That Christmas we attended charitable functions or just sat together in the pub whilst she toyed with her drink. We spent hours in her room talking about the future. Leeds University had held her place open indefinitely and she often talked of taking that place when her treatment ended. The thought of going to Leeds seemed to keep her going during the darkest hours. I never thought that this would ever be a realistic possibility, but then I think I always underestimated her determination.

As the time approached for her to return to Christie the tension within her became palpable. She became irritable and there were moments when I thought that she would refuse to go. When the time came she never refused, and in spite of her tremendous fear, she always tried to put me at my ease.

'I'll be fine, Daddy, it's only four days.'

Four days of pain, nausea, vomiting, fear and doubt; she was certainly more courageous than I could ever be.

She tried to smile as Judy drove her away on that grey January morning. She looked frightened and close to tears, and in spite of two weeks at home, she was still pale yellow and looked very tired. As I waved goodbye I wondered just where she found the will to carry on, to face the pain and trauma of those awful returns to hospital. I missed her dreadfully during those treatment weeks. Whenever she left I would wander around the house like a lost soul. I usually ended up in her bedroom feeling guilty for not being with her. Many times, with the benefit of hindsight, I have tortured myself with the question of whether or not I should have been with her during her treatment and many times I have thought of a hundred reasons as to why I didn't or couldn't make those trips with her. But the truth is usually simple, and the simple truth was that I instinctively felt that she didn't want me there and I was glad because I think I would have found her pain just too heart-rending. Judy carried that awful burden whilst I stayed at home with my guilt.

During January and February 1990 we noticed that although she was still very emaciated, the two-week break between treatments was allowing her to recover enough to start going out. During the second week at home especially, she began to look slightly less haggard and I noticed traces of downy hair growing back on her head. At these times Louise was determined to enjoy herself. She loved buying bright clothes and listening to her music. Most particularly she loved Sinead O'Connor, the controversial Irish rock singer. I think in many ways Louise was able to identify with her. Sinead was very direct and seemingly full of anger and contradictions; she also had a shaved head and distinctive make-up. The two of them did not seem dissimilar. Louise had expressed her admiration for Sinead to an old friend of mine who had worked in the music business some years before.

The post clattered through the letterbox on a grey, wet March morning. Amongst the junk mail and bills was a packet for Louise. The handwriting was spidery and barely legible. It was post-marked London. I went to wake her as usual and as always, she was very tired. Six months of chemotherapy had left her with little or no energy, a completely bald head and a propensity for sleeping for long periods. She drowsily opened the packet and I left her to get on with waking up properly.

Her voice was full of excitement as she summoned me back

from the stairs. I raced back to her room thinking she was going to be sick and had no bowl to hand. I found her sitting up in bed with a photograph of Sinead O'Connor and a tape lying next to it. She was holding two or three sheets of lined exercise book paper which she thrust towards me.

'Daddy, Sinead's invited me to her Manchester concert next month. She wants to meet me. I don't believe it, how does she know about me?'

Derek Staton had not only shown a lot of interest in Louise's musical tastes. He had contacted Sinead O'Connor and had told her of Louise's plight. Something about what he said had touched a chord in this very intense and enigmatic young singer. Anyway, Louise was going to meet somebody who had inspired her and perhaps even offered a role model during the toughest part of her life.

Some weeks later I was sitting with Louise on a warm April evening as the sun streamed through her bedroom window and I remember thinking just how far we had come. Although she was still pale yellow and the dark rings around her eyes spoke of grievous illness, her tremendous spirit was still completely intact. She was laughing excitedly as she tied her bright purple headscarf. It was just one of a vast number of scarves collected during numerous shopping trips; all of which were brightly coloured and eye catching. The drab brown NHS wig had now long been discarded and was displayed on a large plastic luminous skull, nicknamed 'Keith', which sat in the corner of her room.

As she prepared herself I sat quietly contemplating this amazing room thinking just how well it reflected her personality, when the doorbell rang. Kim and Steven were two close friends from sixth form college days and Louise had invited them to join her for the concert in Manchester. I had, as instructed, spoken to Doreen Loader at Ensign Records in London and she had made all the arrangements for this special evening. Upon arrival at the Apollo theatre they were to introduce themselves and afterwards, to proceed to an area backstage to meet Sinead. It was going to be a memorable night in more ways than one.

I saw the four of them off and settled to watch TV with a pack of beers. I anticipated that they would be home by 11 p.m. or so.

At 1.30 a.m. they trooped into the living room. I expected Louise to be tired, but she was bright eyed and bubbly. Everything had gone to plan until the end of the concert, at which point there had been a mix-up. Sinead had left with her vast entourage immediately after the show. She was under the impression that Louise was not there. For some reason she had been told that Louise couldn't make it on that night. When she discovered that Sinead had left Louise became quite upset; one of the tour assistants had observed her angst and telephoned Sinead on her mobile phone. By this time she was heading south down the motorway in a huge coach following an exhausting concert. Sinead's response to hearing of Louise's predicament was to order the coach to be turned around back to Manchester. As a result a very apologetic rock star spent a wonderful thirty minutes with a very happy cancer sufferer.

As Louise related this delightful story I visualised a multitude of road crew, sound men PR people and assorted hangers on, sitting looking in exasperation at their watches and wondering if they would ever get to London that night. Of course, Louise was oblivious to all of that. She was living one day at a time and that moment was all that mattered. Sinead O'Connor was to return to Louise's life in the not too distant future.

The summer of 1990 was mercilessly difficult for Louise. It was a summer of vomiting, of trips to Christie, of weight loss, tranquillisers, angst, fear and pain. But it was also a summer of great security and precious times spent together. We were secure in the knowledge that Louise, in spite of her awful appearance, was not going to die just yet. Her cancer was still being bombarded every third week, but we always knew that we would get her back at the end of that time, even though at times she looked so ill as to be almost unrecognisable. And so for the first week we fed her and nurtured her as one would a small fledgling, and then during that wonderful second week at home we revelled in our intense and joyous times together. Friends visited and small unplanned gatherings became parties that went on long into the night, and sometimes until dawn. Judy christened these 'kitchen parties', and they were wonderful. No time was wasted, everything seemed to have a special significance.

Often during the early hours of Sunday morning I wandered from the kitchen to the living room when most friends had left. The house would be strewn with empty beer cans and wine bottles, and there, amongst the rubble, I would find Louise lying half asleep, head resting on uncle Chris who would invariably be the worse for wear. These were the best of times, but the worst of times were never far away.

★

I think it was about the time of Louise's ninth or tenth chemo-therapy session. She had become very drowsy as usual and woke from a long sleep to see a strange woman sitting at her bedside talking quietly to Nan. She introduced herself to Louise saying her husband had been one of the technicians in attendance during Louise's first operation to investigate the tumour in her instep. She went on to explain that her twenty-year-old son had been suffering from cancer for over a year and that her husband had suggested that they contact our family some months before. They had, however, decided against this not knowing quite how bad Louise's condition might be. She had come from visiting her son on a ward in another part of the hospital, she had brought with her a packet of biscuits and a written message from her son. She talked about her son's illness quietly for a few minutes before Louise realised from the tone of her conversation that he was in fact, now critically ill. The woman gave Louise her best wishes and left her bedside. Later that evening Louise picked up the message, it read: 'Keep smiling, Louise, love Pascal.' Pascal Lam Bard died the following week. The glamorous and wild-spirited boy who had shared that detention with her so many years ago had succumbed to cancer. His parents Gene and Giles Lam Bard were to become close friends and strong allies during our own dark hours.

As the summer drew on so Louise became more and yet more debilitated. The dreaded infections became much less frequent, though, because of our routines and our developing under-standing of what was happening to our daughter's body. Her fear of Christie had developed to the point that she began to vomit on the way to hospital. This was a purely psychological response to her situation. The dread had become so great that she was vomiting in anticipation of her treatment. No matter how much they tried to prevent the awful vomiting they were never able to alleviate or even reduce the frequency of it, and so Louise suffered the indignity of retching and heaving for what to her, must have felt like an eternity. She complained bitterly. She ranted against every aspect of this bloody treatment, but when push came to shove she always got in that car and always assured me that she would be all right. In the end, Christie decided that the only way to ease her suffering would be to render her semi-conscious during her four days of treatment.

It was on the fourth day in Christie, in late August, that I phoned a very drowsy and dilapidated Louise with the news that a local businessman had kindly nominated her to travel on holiday to St Lucia that October. George Baguley, the owner of a local garden centre had been awarded this holiday by a large seed distributor. He decided he would like to donate the holiday to a good cause. The local newspaper sought nominations from members of the public, Louise won hands down. She was thrilled but barely able to speak after four days of treatment. The holiday was for two and she decided to take her German friend Karin. They were to fly from Gatwick in late October.

By October 1990 Dr Rao announced that Louise's chemotherapy would soon be coming to an end. We were all overjoyed but very worried. We were also aware that in time her strength would return, her hair would grow back and she would begin to look, at long last, less like a corpse and more like our daughter. This would, of course, be wonderful. But while the healthy cells in her body were happily regenerating free from toxic intervention, so something much more sinister might well be developing within her, and, without the inhibiting effect of chemotherapy, would be free to continue its dastardly work.

We awoke on that Saturday morning in late October to a dense freezing fog. It was a very beautiful morning as the fog very slowly gave way to pink swirling mists interspersed with short lived shafts of pale pink sun. As the car nudged its way through the denser fog patches towards the station I could feel Louise's excitement growing.

'Just think, Daddy, I'll be lying on a hot Caribbean beach and you'll be stuck here with all this cold and fog.'

I glanced over my shoulder, she was rummaging in her handbag looking for her walkman. She had discarded her headscarf and her head looked for all the world like a light bulb! She was going to spend a week with Karin in St Lucia and then return for a final four days in purgatory.

Karin was flying to London from Germany and we were to meet her at my brother's house that evening. Tim would then drive the girls out to Gatwick to catch the St Lucia flight at seven-thirty the following morning. But for now, I thought, we were going to spend some special father and daughter time together. As we settled into our seats in that freezing railway carriage I took a mental photograph of a very brave and slightly eccentric young woman. Beneath her newly tied purple headscarf her skin was tight around her forehead and cheek bones. Her soft brown eyes were set in a sea of pale yellow and beneath those eyes were bags of deep grey. She was beyond exhaustion now and I wondered if Dr Rao was calling halt to the chemotherapy because her broken body just couldn't take any more. I thought that this short break in the sun would fortify her, and that this last session, in just over a week's time would in some way, be less of an ordeal. I was completely wrong.

As the train moved off through the thick mist and fog I watched her cursing under her breath: 'Fuck these wires,' she muttered as she struggled to untangle her walkman leads from around her left ear, right elbow and neck.

This was Louise at her best. She always seemed to be struggling to untangle or mend something, and it was never her fault. I laughed out loud as the simple tangle became impossibly worse.

'And fuck you as well,' she shouted more audibly as the wire threatened to decapitate her.

People all around fell silent with embarrassment. We began to giggle uncontrollably as she slammed the walkman down on the table.

'I'll have some sweets instead.'

She dived into her bag, rummaging deep through lipsticks, tissues, nail varnish and many more things that she wasn't ever going to need.

'I've forgotten the bloody sweets,' she shouted in disbelief.

She repeated this declaration a number of times. She began to accuse her young brothers of a most heinous theft when there was a shriek from further down the carriage. Nan had boarded the train at the next village to travel the fifteen miles to Preston. She sat down and also began to search her handbag (I am fascinated by the whole subject of women and handbags). Nan produced enough chocolate bars to last for an eternity of journeys between Blackpool and London and Louise was placated. She settled more comfortably and engaged me in debate about what might constitute suitable retribution for Sam and Barney. As she quietly ranted, delighting in thoughts of the most sadistic punishments imaginable, I recalled that I had seen her mountain of sweets on the table by her bed not one hour before!

Louise slept the rest of that journey awakening only as the train shuddered to a halt at Euston. We booked a taxi to take us to Wandsworth and were delighted to discover that the driver hailed from St Lucia. He seemed equally intrigued that Louise was on her way there and a rapport was established during which we learned some very interesting, but quite useless, things about the beautiful island of St Lucia.

That night I watched her as she chattered excitedly with Karin over the dinner table. She needed her bed badly but adrenaline had put her into overdrive. At 10 p.m. she insisted that my brother drove her around the sights of London. By the time she returned she was already partly asleep and made straight for her room. That night I slept fitfully on the settee in front of the glowing embers of a coal fire. I remember waking in the early hours listening to the spitting and grating of the dying fire. It was a strange hour or two that I spent in perfect peaceful contemplation of everything that had happened to us during the last fourteen months. Our lives had been completely turned upside down. We had been faced with an impossibly painful reality, and yet we had survived. Not only that, we had experienced times of great joy during this odyssey. There were times also when I felt that events were being moved by a much higher force and with a very clear purpose. I couldn't establish any clear purpose to all of this, but on that cold frosty night as I watched those dying embers I was not afraid, nor did I feel alone.

At 6.30 a.m. we ventured into the dark and frosty air and, whilst Louise was moaning about not having had enough sleep, we loaded the luggage into my brother's estate car and drove to Gatwick. When we arrived we put the girls in the right queue and as I hugged what was left of Louise I heard her cough. It was a rasping cough, but when I asked her if she was okay she shrugged it off with an unconvincing smile.

'Don't fuss, Daddy, I'm fine.'

She sounded far from convincing and she looked far too tired to be travelling halfway round the world. Oh well, at least it was warm and dry on St Lucia, the cough would probably clear up quite quickly. Tim drove me back for breakfast and offered to drive me into London to do some shopping. I was keen to get home and worried about Louise. I had let her go before but only to Christie and I knew that had I so wanted I could have been with her within the hour. This was different and as I sat on the train I looked disconsolately at the empty seat opposite me and I wanted her back.

The following Wednesday the phone rang at about 8 p.m. It was Louise; she sounded terrible. She had been on St Lucia for just four days and her cough had developed into a chest infection. I cursed myself, I should have known. How the hell could that cough have cleared up, she had no immune system left. As she wheezed and croaked down the telephone I was very concerned.

'I'm fine, Daddy, honestly,' she said. 'I'll be home on Friday and we'll have some larks.'

She sounded breathless and frightened. I told her to find a doctor and explain everything. She was noncommittal and I felt helpless.

She was due to fly to London in two days time. My brother would pick her up from Gatwick and take her to his house for the night. Karin would fly straight on to Germany. I couldn't wait to see her again. Tim phoned late on Friday night, Louise had returned safely. I spoke to her and she still sounded awful. She cursed her luck and then tried to laugh, she only succeeded in coughing violently. I telephoned Christie. They were very concerned about her condition and made arrangements for us to take her straight to Blackpool Victoria Hospital for blood tests and antibiotics as soon as she arrived from London. We picked her up from the railway station on that damp Guy Fawkes night at about 8 p.m. She looked surprisingly well because of her sun tan, but her eyes were sunken and her breathing laboured. She was back home and we were in control again. We drove to the hospital and as the doctor rolled up Louise's sleeve to take blood I realised that she should never have taken that holiday. Her arm was so wasted I feared that they would find no blood in there at all.

As it transpired her blood count was life-threateningly low. The doctor telephoned Christie with the result. She was due to undergo her final treatment in forty-eight hours. Dr Rao was unsure that we could safely go ahead. She had, it seemed, reached an all-time low. The doctor at Victoria had never seen such a low blood count. As we waited at home for Dr Rao to phone us with his decision Louise slumped exhausted in her chair. She must have sensed my watching her for she turned her head wearily towards me, 'Did you ever find those sweets, Daddy?' she said, and with that she fell asleep.

Dr Rao decided to proceed with this last chemotherapy. The break in St Lucia had already meant a week's delay. He had allowed her to spend three weeks at home prior to her holiday in order that she should be stronger. Louise didn't argue. In fact, I sensed that she wanted to get this one over with. And so on 6 November, 1990 she set off to Christie for her final dose of poison. Fourteen months of horrendous and tortuous treatment would soon be at and end and we were frightened.

That last course of treatment was tougher even than we had imagined, and when Louise returned home she was very close to breaking point. Her eyes were full of pain and she was close to tears and shaking with emotion. The vomiting started soon afterwards and as I listened to that pitiful retching and heaving, for the hundredth time I wondered whether it had all been worth it and just how much time we had bought at so high a price.

The only formal contact that we would have with Christie in

the future was to be our monthly visits to see if Louise's cancer was still in remission. This was to be a very different kind of ordeal for Louise, a purely psychological torture with no physical side effects. Every month she had to travel to see Dr Rao to be told whether she was going to live or die.

On that day, though, I don't think that she gave a damn about the future. The vomiting stopped and I heard her shuffling about in her room. There followed a long silence and, as always, I crept up to her room to see how she was. She was in a deep sleep. Her headscarf slipped over to one side and her long bony fingers clutching a tissue. I sat down on the bed and held her hand. She had come such a long way in such a very short time, and it showed. The relatively naïve young girl who was told she had cancer fourteen months ago had been transformed into one of the toughest young women I had ever met. She had been to hell and back not once but many times and it showed. Death had been hovering dangerously in the background all the while, but it was now time for him to take a back seat. He wasn't having her just yet.

By Christmas 1990 she looked markedly stronger. The waxen yellow skin became less pallid and tinged with pink. She began to put on weight and was able to wear her rings again. But most importantly I noticed that her hair was growing back and her face was slightly less drawn. As the toxins left her body so she returned to occupy it. She retained the bright make-up that had become something of a trade mark, but now it looked less like a mask and more a part of her.

Christmas that year was a proper celebration as the real Louise began to emerge from the wreckage. Dressed in her black leather studded jacket and Doc Martens she began to exude something resembling energy for the first time in over a year. The sparkle returned to her eyes and friends began to talk of recovery and miracles. We knew better, however, and began to mentally prepare for the long hard road ahead.

Chapter Four

In January 1991 Louise went back to Christie for the dreaded monthly check-up. Each month Judy drove her to Manchester while I stayed at home to look after the boys and await that terrible phone call. Would she be all-clear or would she be given a death warrant? On that January morning I paced the living room floor with a knotted stomach, sweating palms and cigarettes. Whenever the telephone rang I snatched at it, heart racing and then with growing irritation tried to explain to the tele-sales person that I didn't want anything. Eventually, after about two hours, the call came and I could almost feel the relief in Judy's voice, 'Everything's okay,' she said, and I collapsed on the stairs in relief.

We had another month. Another month to help her grow stronger, another month to live one day at a time. I poured a drink and noticed that my hand was shaking violently.

By early spring of 1991 we had had two or three 'all-clears' and Louise began to blossom. She had returned to her full weight and was brimming with confidence and plans for the future. Her hair was cropped short and much darker than before chemotherapy. On 2 March, 1991 we awoke to a light covering of snow. Louise was delighted, snow was always special to her, but more important even than the snow was the fact that today was her twentieth birthday. Birthdays for her had become like landmarks, small victories in this endless battle with cancer.

We were planning a very special day when the doorbell rang and Judy shouted upstairs, 'There's a delivery for you, Louise.'

Judy came into the room carrying a huge basket of champagne and chocolates. In one corner was a small envelope. She loved surprises and didn't hurry to open the envelope. My immediate thought was that Uncle Chris had come up on the horses and in a moment of drunken sincerity had spent the lot on this magnificent display. The card read: 'Have a wonderful birthday,

Louise, with love, Sinead, John and Jake'. Louise was incredulous and a little bewildered. Sinead O'Connor was heading both the single and the album charts that week. She was being ferried frantically from concert to concert all around the world. In spite of this she had thought of Louise, a young cancer victim living in a provincial northern town in the middle of nowhere. Little did we know just how much she was thinking of her at that time.

About a week later and following another 'all-clear' from Christie the phone rang. Doreen Loader (from Sinead's recording company) asked if Louise and I would be interested in coming down to London for a day to have lunch with John Reynolds (Sinead O'Connor's husband) and to spend the day at Ensign Records in Bayswater. Doreen had been responsible for making all the arrangements the previous year for Louise to see Sinead's concert in Manchester. On the telephone she had come across as a very warm and kind person who seemed particularly moved by Louise's plight and, I sensed, was quite keen to meet her. We agreed at once, we were curious to meet people who were so close to this very talented and outspoken young singer, and in any case Louise was well and a day out in London was precisely what we needed.

On 26 March we settled into our seats bound for London. How different, I thought, as I watched her delving into her handbag for her chocolate, from that trip to London six months before. Her face was now filled out completely, she radiated good health, her skin glowed and her eyes were bright. She was wearing her leather motorcycle jacket (a present from Uncle Chris) and black and white harlequin leggings, outrageous earrings and red Doc Marten boots. Moreover, instead of falling asleep on the journey she kept up an animated conversation for almost four hours. The adrenaline was pumping with anticipation. She loved meeting new people and this day was going to be special. As she talked I cast my mind back to that dreadful day in 1989 when Dr Rao had told us she was going to die. I shuddered in disbelief as if recalling a nightmare and then I put those thoughts away. 'One day at a time, Philip, one day at a time', I was going to enjoy today and nothing else mattered.

The taxi pulled up outside a small three storey building in a sort of back street. It wasn't very salubrious, more Dickensian. We pressed a button and Doreen's unmistakable London lilt beckoned us in from the top floor. The door buzzed and clicked and I can remember climbing the steep stairs to emerge into a brightly lit reception area to be greeted by a charming young woman of about Louise's age. Elaine was Doreen's assistant and immediately struck me as someone who I would not expect to be sitting at the reception desk of a record company. She was open and very natural. There was no hint of the slickness and artificiality that I would have expected from somebody doing such a job – especially in London!

Doreen came out to greet us. She was in her late fifties, blonde, slim and well dressed. Again I expected toughness, platitudes and for Louise to be patronised in a kind of 'does she take sugar' way. Doreen was nothing like what we expected. She was one of the warmest, kindest and, yes, shrewdest people I had ever met. Louise loved her from the outset, and as I watched them talking I sensed that this woman was going to stick around in Louise's life. I was not to be disappointed.

John Reynolds came into Doreen's small office with a brown package under his arm. He was in his late twenties and a drummer in Sinead's backing band. Again, he did not fit the stereotype. He was self-effacing, quite shy and really quite ordinary, dressed in jeans and a conventional leather jacket. He presented Louise with the parcel and invited her to open it. As she was struggling with the string and sellotape I noticed John wink at Doreen and wondered if the parcel contained some sort of practical joke. It seemed to take an age, but eventually she ripped away the cardboard casing and I noted a flash of glass and silver. As she examined the contents I noticed her eyes began to fill up. She turned around and hugged John and then turned back to me. She held up her half-wrapped trophy.

'Daddy look,' she demanded.

She was holding a framed platinum disc, there was an inscription above the disc itself that read 'Presented to Louise to recognise the sales in the United Kingdom of more that 600,000 copies of the Ensign single "Nothing Compares 2 U" 1990'. Sinead had given Louise her platinum disc. Louise was thrilled.

The rest of that day was spent having lunch in a Thai restaurant and just being around the Ensign office. Louise loved every minute. This was a different world for her. Thus far she had known only school and hospital. This was heady stuff indeed, listening to Doreen negotiating contracts with rock bands and hearing tales of Sinead and her climb from suburban Dublin to stardom. All around were framed discs and posters. This was a world to which Louise would return time and again. We took a late train home that night sharing a pack of beer and an empty carriage. We were soon sleeping contentedly heading back to reality and 'one day at a time'.

I remember that I was pottering about in the front garden on a very warm late spring afternoon when the phone rang. Louise was shopping in town and I fully expected to be explaining that to one of her friends when I picked up the receiver. The small Irish voice seemed quite distant at first and then the line cleared: 'Could I speak to Louise, please,' the tone was almost apologetic.

I told the caller that she was out shopping and asked who was calling.

'It's Sinead here, I'm sorry to bother you, I'm phoning from Los Angeles; can I call back later?'

I was taken aback. I made small talk for a minute or so and she asked how Louise was and expressed admiration for her. I arranged that she should call back at 5.30 p.m. GMT.

Louise burst through the front door with customary energy and began to relate some amusing incident that had occurred on the bus home.

'You had a call earlier, Louise,' I tried to sound matter of fact.

She barely acknowledged this apparently mundane piece of information before continuing with her story, 'so when Kim got off the bus…'

'It was Sinead O'Connor calling from Los Angeles, she's calling back at 5.30 p.m.'

'You really are quite sad, aren't you, Daddy?'

I just stared back at her.

'Okay she didn't,' I said. 'I just made it up because I'm so sad and lonely.'

She was hooked.

'You're serious aren't you?'

I repeated the message and Louise became excited. Louise went up to her room to wait for her call.

'If you're lying, Daddy...'

She sounded quite threatening.

I heard the telephone ring and Louise take the call in her room. From the living room I could hear Louise's response as her voice became quite excited. I can't remember how long the call lasted but I certainly remember Louise bounding down the stairs two at a time. Sinead had invited her to spend some time in London the following month. She would meet Louise at Euston and they would spend a few days together. Louise was incredulous. She had been happy just to meet Sinead O'Connor the previous year, and to have received the platinum disc, but now she was on her way to stay with her.

We drove her to the station on a bright sunny late April morning. She had been given her fourth all-clear and cancer was far from our thoughts as we checked tickets, money and went through that well rehearsed routine so familiar to parents the world over.

'Now, are you sure she's going to be at Euston, if she's not there just stay where you are and ring Doreen – and behave yourself!'

With all such rituals completed she boarded the train for London and we returned home satisfied that she had taken enough clothes and money for a twelve month stay in London, never mind four days. She phoned us, as promised as soon as she arrived at Sinead's house in Bayswater. I can only remember that they were planning to go out for a pizza or something and that they were enjoying one another's company. She certainly seemed to have settled in very quickly.

Louise really enjoyed that time in London going to concerts and pizza restaurants. Playing 'Super Mario Brothers' on Sinead's Nintendo, eating onion soup and jaffa cakes at 2 a.m. and spending time with Jake, Sinead's three-year-old son. When she returned she somehow seemed just a little more grown up. The make-up and nail varnish all purple, blue and black and her manner a little more confident. Moreover, Sinead had shaved her head one night when they had been drinking. She looked stunning.

In the weeks following that visit she talked a lot about Sinead's world. I think that she loved the person but was very uncomfortable in the world of the rock star.

'She's surrounded by bullshit, Daddy, I really feel sorry for her.'

Louise had grown up fast, she knew instinctively what was real and important and what was not. She sensed that Sinead was unhappy and she felt helpless to help her. I thought it strange that a young woman with cancer should feel pity for a wealthy and very famous young rock star.

★

I think we read in the local paper that Princess Diana was coming to Blackpool that summer. Anyway, Judy had decided to write to her on a wet February afternoon. Even if she said no then nothing was lost and at least we could say that we had tried. I actually can remember posting that letter in the middle of a wet snow storm. I recall thinking that it was rather eccentric to write to the Princess of Wales asking her to change her schedule to meet Louise. After all, why should Louise matter to her? Nonetheless, I posted the letter and quickly forgot all about it. There were many more important things to attend to that day. Louise was three months out of chemotherapy and we were starting to have fun together.

We received a reply a couple of weeks later from Patrick Jephson, Diana's private secretary. He thanked us for our letter, pointed out that the Princess was on rather a tight schedule and left it there. He did not commit himself to anything, but neither did he say no. I wasn't hopeful, but I never was (cancer had made sure of that), and in any case Louise was growing stronger by the day and we were happy. I have to say that I didn't much care whether she met Diana or not. The fund-raising was going unbelievably well and Louise's image was becoming quite well known in West Lancashire and beyond. Yes, the press really had handled things well, even the photographs were good. Our message had been delivered well, 'strong young woman with cancer – helping others – determination – courage – tragedy'. The money was rolling in, we were going to fulfil our dream after all. I didn't have much time to consider that letter from St James's Palace – we had targets to achieve.

It was a very hot early May morning in 1991 when I was rudely awoken by the telephone next to my bed. Louise was staying in Germany and my first thoughts were for her. Was something wrong? The man from the Lord Lieutenant's office didn't beat about the bush. On Tuesday 2 July we would be meeting the Princess of Wales at Blackpool Town Hall at 1 p.m. He asked me not to contact the press and apart from close family and friends I was to tell no one. At first I couldn't take it in. I had never considered the possibility that this might actually happen. Our request must have been amongst thousands. Why Louise?

Judy was incredulous, in two months time we would be meeting the most famous, and in many ways, controversial woman in the world. I phoned Louise in Germany. She was overjoyed. It didn't matter why Diana had decided that she wanted to meet Louise, she just had and that was enough for all of us. I was pleased that after all that suffering the balance was tipping back in my daughter's favour, albeit temporarily. Little did I know just how significant this first meeting was to be!

I spent the rest of that morning in something of a spin. How long would we spend with her? Would we be alone? What would we talk about? Would I make a fool of myself? Would we be allowed to take her photograph? Photographs, yes, I had to have a photograph at least, even if everything else went right, I had to have a photograph! I phoned the Lord Lieutenant's office and spoke to my contact there. Could I take a small camera to our meeting just to take a few shots? I'm sure Diana wouldn't mind. I tried to sound matter of fact, to convince him that there couldn't possibly be any reason for him to refuse. His response was negative and even quite cagey. He very much doubted that Diana would grant such a request, but he would contact St James's Palace anyway. It was a 'don't hold your breath' sort of response. I put down the phone. Oh well, I had to try.

Twenty minutes later the telephone rang. I expected a bland response containing words like 'sorry' or 'not appropriate'. The man from the Lord Lieutenant's office sounded quite chirpy. He's enjoying this, I thought.

'Her Royal Highness would have no objection to your taking a few photographs.'

If I had had my wits about me I would have hastened to the bookmakers and placed a large bet on the next race – I just couldn't lose that day!

David Cooper called that morning. He couldn't believe our luck. The implication for our charity work would be enormous. The ensuing publicity associated with this visit would be tremendous. Our cause would be placed very much in the spotlight which was exactly what we had been trying to achieve for the last eighteen months. We didn't realise at the time just how strong that spotlight would be nor how long we would spend under its magical glare.

Tuesday 2 July was one of the hottest days of the year. I woke with a jolt at 6 a.m., dressed in jeans and T-shirt and went out onto the patio to contemplate this very special day. My stomach was tense as I thought yet again about what could go wrong. Some weeks earlier we had received written details from the Lord Lieutenant's office. The car would pick us up at 12.30 p.m. to take us to the Town Hall, but there was no mention of how long we were to spend with her, or anything else for that matter. It all seemed very open ended. All this increased my feelings of apprehension; I didn't like not knowing things. We couldn't function well that morning, housework remained untouched and children unfed. Higher things like 'will they forget to pick us up' preoccupied us.

By mid morning the temperature was in the high seventies and black clouds were building in the far distance. Louise remained in bed and I decided to take a walk to calm my nerves. The sun burned hotter and thunder rumbled ominously over the Irish Sea. By the time I returned home Louise was up and about. She showed no nerves and was busily rummaging about amongst the debris in the kitchen looking for something to eat. This was going to be her day and she was savouring every moment.

Just before midday I changed into a dark suit and immediately began to perspire heavily. The temperature was by now into the eighties and the humidity was almost at saturation point. Louise went upstairs to change and put on her make-up and I was left alone to smoke yet another calming cigarette. I was concerned that Louise wouldn't be ready on time, she was notorious for taking her time, especially where make-up was concerned.

I was standing in the hall when I noticed a long dark shadow slide past the front door and come to a halt outside the house. As the chauffeur rang the doorbell I shouted upstairs to Louise. She appeared at the top of the stairs looking beautiful. He skin glowed, her bright make-up shone as she smiled confidently, 'I'm ready, Daddy, let's go.'

The chauffeur held open the door and Judy and Louise climbed into the cool capacious leather rear of the limousine. I jumped into the front and checked my watch. 12.40pm we were not going to be late after all. All morning I had convinced myself that, like the white rabbit in *Alice in Wonderland*, I was certain to be late for our date with a princess.

As the car approached town I noticed that there was a smattering of people lining the pavement. That smattering quickly became a throng as we turned down the road approaching the Town Hall. For the first time in my life I knew what it was like to be famous. People craned their necks as we approached our destination. Cameras flashed as people jostled towards our car. As I got out people leaned forward expectantly. They were bitterly disappointed, for Diana was yet to arrive. In that short time I decided that I didn't want to be famous after all. I didn't really like being the centre of that much attention for even a short time. It felt somehow threatening, as if everybody wanted a piece of me. I was happy to remain a high school teacher. I didn't envy Diana at all.

We were shown into a small upstairs room overlooking the main square. I clearly remember looking down on the vast multi-coloured crowd below and feeling rather superior. They were going to get a glimpse, we were getting much much more. The room was quite dark and comfortably furnished with a fabric-covered settee and two easy chairs. In one corner there was a small table laden with delicious looking food and drink. Food was, however, the furthest thing from my mind at that time.

As I stood in the window overlooking Talbot Square I noticed to my left over the sea black ominous clouds were gathering ever thicker. Simultaneously there was a piercing crack followed by a boom. As the storm started I noticed a green Jaguar slip quietly down an approach road accompanied by police outriders and camera flashes. Diana was arriving and I was scared.

The Jaguar pulled up about fifty metres short of the Town Hall and to everyone's surprise Diana emerged from the back seat to be greeted by a loud raucous cheer. Almost at once huge thunder fed raindrops began to tumble earthwards. Brolleys were opened in unison making the crowd below resemble a kaleidoscope of bright colour. One of Diana's aides opened a huge golf umbrella in a vain attempt to protect her from the rain. She moved quickly to the crowd hand outstretched as the aide scurried behind desperately trying the keep up with her as she weaved her way along the crash barriers. The police looked nervous, the crowd was ecstatic.

By the time she returned to her car she was soaked to the skin. The car moved very slowly towards the Town Hall entrance until it was directly below my feet. There was a quiet knock on our door and Patrick Jephson, Diana's private secretary, introduced himself.

'Her Royal Highness will be with you shortly,' he said.

He had a few words with Louise and left us alone to await her entrance. Within seconds the door burst open and a very wet Princess of Wales opened the conversation as she moved quickly towards Louise.

'Hi, you must be Louise, I'm so pleased to meet you.'

Louise was not in the least fazed by the informality and sheer *joie de vivre* of this amazing young woman. I was immediately struck dumb. She was breathtakingly beautiful and seemed to fill that small room with her presence. But I was not in awe of her, more, I think, drawn to her. She was very warm and her body language was open and welcoming. In short, even during that first few seconds she had made me feel good about myself, even quite important. Everyone likes to feel like that and she had the gift of making you feel special. Within two minutes we were feeling comfortable with her.

She collapsed on the settee and patted the cushions beckoning Louise to sit beside her.

'I'm sorry I look like a drowned rat,' she said, 'but I'm visiting the blind home next – at least they won't notice.'

She started to giggle like a schoolgirl and Louise joined in. This was mildly irreverent and Louise loved irreverence. Diana gestured for me to sit in one of the easy chairs and Judy did likewise. I found myself sitting within two or three feet of her, and whilst she was getting to know Judy and Louise I started to notice lots of things about her. My senses moved into overdrive as I began to relax. Her clothes were immaculately cut. She was wearing a red jacket and red and white striped skirt, which struck me as being both tight and short. Her jewellery was not ostentatious but subdued and delicate. She was fine boned; her skin radiated good health, tight around the cheekbones and deep brown. Her legs were long and a little too well muscled. Her hair was wet and sticking to her forehead which was completely unlined. Diana had the most beautifully crystal clear penetrating blue eyes, and behind those eyes there was a smile that generated great warmth. From the moment of our first meeting her eyes transfixed me. She flirted, she made jokes, she became immensely serious and the eyes reflected everything. She showed an array of her emotions that day and I sensed her vulnerability, for I felt she was far too honest for her own good.

We talked for a long time about Louise and her fund-raising, and I remember vividly her questions to Louise about her illness. Most notably, early on in our meeting, she asked Louise how angry she was. Many people had broached the subject of Louise's cancer with her but none had addressed her anger. Anger was the overriding emotion in all of us, but something we had not openly discussed. This young woman certainly had a way of getting to the heart of things very quickly, she undoubtedly possessed an acute intelligence. Louise soon realised that Diana didn't deal in platitudes and euphemism and the conversation quickly became intimate as the two of them laughed and joked and began to enjoy one another's company. I remember thinking during that amazing hour that it wasn't supposed to be like this. This was the future

Queen of England, so why was she giggling like a schoolgirl with Judy and Louise? Was she always like this? I cannot answer that last question but during subsequent meetings and phone calls I found this incredible young woman to be one of the warmest and most honest people I had ever met.

By the end of our time with her that day it seemed that we had covered so many things. Judy and Diana talked for quite a while about Prince William's accident with a golf club. Judy related her experiences of hospital waiting rooms and of motherhood in general. Diana was passionate about her boys and very keen to know how ordinary mothers like Judy cope with accidents and everyday 'being a mother' things. She talked warmly of Charles and seemed interested by my experiences working as a social worker with disaffected and deprived young people. Everything we said seemed to interest her and she genuinely appeared to be enjoying herself. She was certainly very taken by Louise, especially her story of how she had come to acquire her priceless platinum disc from Sinead earlier that year. Diana told Louise that it was her favourite record but that she only had the plastic version!

As the conversation flowed the skies outside darkened. I could hear the thunder rumbling outside until finally there was an almighty crack almost overhead and all the alarms in the Town Hall seemed to go off at once. Security men burst into the room; she remained seated but did not ask them to leave. I sensed she was about to return to her crowd who were patiently waiting outside in torrential rain. As she made to leave I asked her if she would come back the following year to open the Day Hospice which we had worked so hard to help build.

'Write to me Philip,' she said. 'I'll see.'

At least she didn't say no. As she was ushered out of the room she looked over her shoulder at me: 'For God's sake don't have the photos developed at Boots.'

I had completely forgotten that Judy had taken six photographs; Diana had been so utterly captivating.

I don't remember anything about the journey home except that just before getting in the car I hurriedly handed a photographer friend the film from Judy's camera. We arrived home to unwashed dishes and a feeling of unreality. It was just not possible that fifteen minutes before we had been enjoying an intimate and lengthy conversation with the future Queen of England, and here we were in our very ordinary kitchen facing the prospect of the previous day's washing-up. I felt hungry and tired and noticed that a little of the sparkle had gone from Louise. The day had taken more out of us than we thought. The washing-up could wait.

★

As I stood in the queue at Tesco waiting to pay for my pizzas and beer I tried to reflect upon that extraordinary meeting. Louise and Diana had taken to each other immediately. It was just as if they had known one another all their lives. They were both naturally warm and charismatic young women, and Diana, as I was to later discover, was suffering a great deal of anguish and emotional pain in her private life. As time went by I often wondered if that was why they felt they had so much in common. Could they instinctively have sensed one another's pain on that hot thundery day?

We spent the rest of that memorable day comparing notes and trying to recall things in more detail. We all agreed that we expected the Princess of Wales to be far more formal. We were surprised that we had been allowed to be alone with her for so long, and that she had become so intimate so quickly. Her spontaneity and charm had taken us completely by surprise. But it was a wonderful surprise. She was certainly physically very beautiful, but flawed like all true beauty. I remember thinking that her nose was bent noticeably to the right of her face and was perhaps a little too long. I also noticed that she smelled of fresh rain. She didn't seem to be wearing any perfume.

The experience of meeting Diana made an indelible impression on all of us, but it was far from the impression we expected. We could not have dreamed at that time just how much better we were to get to know this enigmatic, hugely vulnerable and very complex young woman.

Chapter Five

The fund-raising was going from strength to strength. Diana's visit to us resulted in an upsurge of donations and by the late summer of 1991 we were rapidly approaching our £100,000 target. We were involved in one charitable function after another, and every so often we met David Cooper to have a look at the foundations and scaffolding that was the Day Hospice. Louise began to be recognised in the street and every week brought letters from well-wishers and cheques to boost our cause. The most moving of these were from young people with whom Louise was closely identified. Our work was largely aimed at young people and our message was effectively that young people get cancer too. It was a stark message but it hit home as schools and other organisations pledged to our cause.

It was late July and I was dozing in bed promising to get up. Louise sauntered into the room and sat on the end on my bed as usual. I asked her what she fancied doing later and she seemed a little distracted.

'Daddy you know how I've been clear now for nearly seven months?'

I think I knew what was coming next.

'Well, I think I'll take my place at Leeds this September.'

It was like a bombshell. I knew it had been on her mind for some time. Wendy her social worker from Christie had broached the subject with me once or twice, but I had never considered that it was a serious possibility. She was, after all, terminally ill. But of course she didn't know that. This left me in a quandary. Shall I tell her that she can't go because she's dying? Of course not. But I *can't* let her go because she *is* dying. Her cancer could return at any time and then I'll lose her. I can't have her spending priceless time at university that she could be spending with us!

Wendy visited and we all sat down with Louise to discuss the feasibility of her taking her university place that autumn. It was obvious from the outset that Wendy and Louise had been discussing this possibility for some time. They had both decided that it would be a very positive move to allow Louise to take her place. I suppose in many ways we were presented with a *fait accompli*. There was little we could do, after all Louise was twenty years old and very much her own woman. And so it was resolved, in spite of my objections, that on 30 September she would travel to Leeds to begin a new life. She was delighted and I was apprehensive. I had no choice but to let her go but it didn't stop me trying to dissuade her. I tried every tactic: 'university is over rated,' 'students are so bloody pretentious' and then in desperation, 'why don't you leave it for another year?' She merely smiled and continued to pack her things and prepare for her move to Charles Morris hall of residence. She was off to Leeds University to study single honours German and it was going to be the experience of a lifetime. The child of fairies and goblins had become a beautiful and very bright young woman who was asserting her independence. She was finally leaving home.

The summer of 1991 was hot and very busy as far as Louise was concerned. Following the Princess's visit Louise travelled back to London to spend a few more days with Sinead and her son Jake. It was her son's fourth birthday and there was to be a party for him. Louise went down to help out. She returned north more convinced then ever that the world of the rock star was not real enough for her, it was all too pretentious and shallow. Following her long ordeal she had no time for whimsy or passing fads. She was rooted very much in reality and didn't easily disguise her disdain and annoyance at what she termed 'bullshit'.

This was well illustrated by an incident which occurred during Jake's birthday party. During Louise's first visit she had met a very large black man called Winston. He seemed to accompany Sinead almost everywhere. His role seemed to be that of a minder or bodyguard. From the outset Louise instinctively didn't like him, apart from anything else she felt he was quiet to the point of rudeness. As time went by Louise decided that this dislike was mutual. She felt that Winston was weighing her up and forming a poor opinion of her. In short, they hardly ever spoke. During Jake's party Louise identified a particularly loud-mouthed woman who was determined to gain centre stage. As the woman became louder and more obnoxious so Louise felt drawn to take her on; she was also conscious of the fact that she was a guest in Sinead's house and so she tried to restrain herself. Finally, this woman decided, perhaps because she was aware of Louise's presence, to denounce people from the north of England and northern England in general. This was too much. Louise was justifiably proud of her heritage. She proceeded to verbally lacerate this poor woman, so much so that the woman left the party in tears.

As Louise moved away from the scene of victory she felt a hand on her shoulder and, thinking that she was about to be engaged in another argument, turned sharply to see Winston smiling from ear to ear and holding out a drink.

'That was fantastic, Louise. I've waited ages to see that happen, the woman has had it coming for so long, she's so full of shit – well done!'

It was the first time she had heard Winston speak, let alone smile. He became her constant companion for the rest of that holiday. I relate this merely to illustrate an important part of my daughter's character. Her approach to people was almost always gentle and considerate, but every now and again she came up against malevolence or prejudice and felt duty-bound to respond.

Doreen invited her to spend a week or so working at Ensign that August. Louise snatched the opportunity with both hands and within ten days of returning from Sinead's she was back on the train to Euston and her room at my brother's house in Wandsworth. She adored working at Ensign with Doreen and Elaine. Meeting bands, taking calls, making tea and laughing. She shared her outrageous sense of humour with Doreen, and whenever they were together there was laughter. Her time in London became a social whirl. Each night she went to rock concerts or to see new bands with Doreen. They were inseparable during that time and that bond was to endure for the rest of Louise's life.

*

Late September came around quickly and I prepared myself mentally for her departure at the end of that month. The charity continued to prosper and Louise continued to pack her bags in readiness for leaving on the thirtieth. We began to walk into Poulton together quite regularly and as the leaves began to fall on those beautiful balmy afternoons, so I began to hope against hope that Dr Rao had been wrong after all. She had grown up so much by now. She was mellow, thoughtful and full of a charm that people around her found very attractive.

Those last few days at home are forever stamped on my memory. We spent a lot of time with Uncle Chris. We wandered to the pub to sit and talk. But mostly we reflected on a marvellous year of Diana and London and best of all ten 'all-clears' from Christie. I think we were closer during that 'leaving time' than we had ever been, and I think Louise felt the same. We spent hour upon hour talking about her childhood. So often conversations started with 'Daddy, do you remember when…' Sometimes we just sat in silence savouring a moment. At that time cancer seemed like just a bad dream.

And so on Sunday 30 September, 1991 we loaded the car with case upon case and bag upon bag until it could take no more, and drove over the Pennines to Leeds. Of course, Leeds was easy to find and once there finding the University was a doddle, every sign seemed to point to it. The trouble was that the University seemed to cover about a half of the city and once we had arrived in Leeds we spent the best part of half an hour literally driving around in circles looking for Charles Morris hall of residence. Eventually, we noticed a large group of parents tearfully bidding their embarrassed offspring goodbye. We parked the car and walked through this ill assorted group and into the entrance to the large block of flats that was to become Louise's home from home.

We were greeted by a number of fresh-faced students who had probably undergone the same ritual this time last year as new students. Of course, they were now full of confidence having worked out where the bar was and how to find their way to their rooms without getting lost. One such student was being consulted by anxious parents and pointing confidently this way and that. She was also holding a list, which seemed to confer proper authority. List consulted, we loaded Louise's belongings into a tiny lift and, there being no more room in the lift, I began to ascend the cold dark concrete stairs that led to the fourth floor. I heard Louise well before I saw her. The voice was emanating from behind a navy blue door at the end of a corridor off to my right.

'Mummy, it's wonderful,' her voice was overflowing with excitement.

I found them standing in a tiny room about nine feet by nine. Louise was busy pulling the folding bed out of the wall, making the room even smaller. The room had brick walls and a panoramic view towards Leeds United football ground. Louise was in seventh heaven.

'What do you think, Daddy?'

'I think it's a load of crap, Louise, you're coming home, you can't possible live in this, it's far too small!'

Louise's eyes flashed and for a moment I felt much as the loud-mouthed woman in London must have done. She didn't say anything but began to open her suitcase. By the time she had arranged her oranges (a present from Uncle Chris's mum) into a fruit bowl I knew I had lost. I really did want her not to like that room, and I would happily have taken her home there and then, but I could see that she was impatient to be rid of us. She had things to do, places to explore and people to meet. She looked at me in an 'oh, Daddy you're such an arse' kind of way and then threw her arms around my neck.

'Daddy, I'll phone you tonight, now please go home.'

There was an exasperated tone in her voice and I felt like a fussy old woman. As I walked back down those dingy concrete stairs I felt the first tears prick around my eyes. As I made my way back towards the car through groups of parents saying goodbye to their healthy offspring I began to feel angry.

'I promise I'll look after the ponies, Fiona.' At least Fiona will be coming home in one piece, I thought. I sat in the car and began to cry.

Judy and I didn't speak much on the way home but I can remember secretly wishing that Louise would get homesick and come home so that I could be needed again. We had been home for about an hour when the telephone rang. She didn't even introduce herself she was fizzing with excitement.

'Daddy, it's so brilliant here; I've met most of the girls on my landing and we've just been to the bar.'

She was breathless with happiness.

'I haven't got lectures for a few days so I'm going to have a good time.'

She spoke to Judy for a while and I heard the usual parental concerns expressed – 'make sure you keep warm, don't lose your key, don't spend all your money, don't drink too much.' Louise disregarded most of that advice during the first week alone!

Each night Louise telephoned and each time something new had happened in her life. She made many new friends and was voted by the girls on her floor to represent them on some staff/student forum. She joined the Irish Society because they held regular nights in a rather fine pub, went to discos and parties or just spent long evenings talking and drinking with her friends in the communal kitchen at the end of her corridor. She befriended her next door neighbour, a German girl called Annette. Louise adapted very quickly to this new hectic life, but she always kept in touch.

After three weeks I could wait no longer, I phoned Uncle Chris and asked him if he fancied going over to Leeds to see Louise the following Sunday. We picked him up at about 10 a.m. on a warm late October morning. I was a little apprehensive as we drove over the Pennines to Leeds. After all those excited phone calls describing this wonderful new life, I just didn't know what to expect. We had arranged to meet Louise on the steps outside her hall of residence at 1 p.m. I was immediately anxious when she wasn't there; I feared something terrible had happened and began to berate Chris. She appeared smiling from the dining room and as she did I chastised her for being late. I realised afterwards that the last two years had changed me more than I thought. I had come to expect to find problems in everything, the simple matter of Louise being a few minutes late had in my mind, become a minor catastrophe. I knew that I had become over protective.

We drove a few miles out of Leeds and spent a delightful afternoon in a comfy pub. By the time we returned to the hall of residence it was almost dark. Chris and I walked up those dark concrete steps whilst Judy, Louise and Barney took the lift. Her room was a revelation. In just over three weeks the depressing little square of brick and breeze block had been transformed completely. TV, stereo, post cards, posters, rugs and an ubiquitous bowl of oranges sitting in the window. The room was now warm, bright and welcoming. It reflected perfectly Louise's personality, and for the first time since she left home I felt content.

Louise took us into the landing's communal area having warned Chris and I about our behaviour, 'Just don't embarrass me, Daddy.'

Of course I proceeded to do exactly that.

'Do you remember when you were four, Louise, and you used to call me King Goblin?'

Her eyes flashed, her friends began to giggle and then she decided to go with the flow. As we prepared to leave I noticed that Louise's status within the group was high. The other students seemed to defer to her. They were never obsequious but they seemed to hold her in high esteem. They knew of her cancer and I think that they were in awe of what she represented and what she had achieved.

It was dark as we pulled away and as I watched her standing on those vast steps clutching the twenty pound note that Chris had given her I thought just how vulnerable she was. At that moment she looked awfully alone. I knew that cancer was never far away. Just waiting in the wings to make another entrance, to claim her back. I made a conscious effort to put such thoughts away. None of us ever has more than today. Today she is okay, nothing else matters. 'One day at a time, Philip, one day at a time.'

*

As autumn slowly changed to winter the joyous phone calls continued and we had another Sunday in Leeds with her (Chris's mother adding generously to the hoard of oranges). Whenever I prompted her or openly suggested that she visit us she always argued some prior social engagement, she loved her freedom in Leeds. One evening in mid-November Louise telephoned, she sounded a little tired.

'Can I bring Annette home for the weekend, Daddy?'

I was happy to agree even though it was Friday and she was

planning to travel immediately to Poulton by train. Judy made up a bed and I began to feel unsettled. There was no sparkle in her voice, she must be tired after a long week of studying.

The train was due to arrive in Poulton at about 8 p.m. It was more than two hours late. I quietly cursed as I waited on the platform in the frost and fog. She would be exhausted by now, I thought, why couldn't she have left it until the morning? As the train emptied its two or three exhausted passengers into the night I became quickly anxious; she wasn't there. I walked through the thick fog towards the end of the long train and felt considerable relief to hear two voices conversing in German. My relief was short lived as Louise appeared through the fog with Annette. She was limping and breathing quite heavily. She looked pale and worried. Her eyes were dull and I sensed that she was in pain. I took her suitcase and asked her how she felt, 'I'm fine, Daddy,' she smiled, but she was fooling no one.

Half an hour later we were sitting comfortably listening to the gentle hiss of the gas fire. Louise and Annette were lounging on the floor in front of us. Louise was visibly brighter now, but I was still feeling a little apprehensive. It was a feeling born of instinct. Louise and I were always very aware of even the smallest change in one another's mood or feelings, and on that night I simply couldn't settle. I knew that she had something to tell me, but I didn't know how to encourage her, and a part of me didn't want to. In a flash of inspiration I asked the girls if they wanted a drink; alcohol always made Louise much less inhibited and more talkative. I went to the kitchen. I couldn't believe my eyes, for the first time in years we didn't have a drop of alcohol in the house. I looked at the clock and it was almost midnight. I wasn't to be beaten, the pub was only two minutes away. I was sure that Tony, the landlord would still be up, and, after all, this was an emergency.

As I walked through the fog I was relieved to see the bar lights still on and more relieved still to see Tony and his wife busily emptying ash trays and replacing beer mats. I tapped on the window. Tony came to the front door and I explained my predicament.

'I can let you have a bottle of scotch, come down to the cellar.'

He was smiling as he walked towards me carrying a one gallon bottle of Bells. 'Is this enough?' he said and began to laugh.

And so it was that a puzzled looking policeman slowed down his patrol car to inspect more closely a man walking tentatively across an icy pavement carrying a gallon of scotch whisky at quarter past midnight!

Louise drank the glass of neat whisky quickly and began to look thoughtful. I could feel the tension building.

'Daddy, I've got a small lump in my groin, about the size of a pea.'

I froze, I was sure that this was an indication that her cancer had returned. I felt my stomach tighten and felt my heart racing. I hadn't felt like this since her last 'all-clear' a month before when she had taken the train from Leeds to Manchester to have her check up alone. We'd had ten months cancer free and I felt cheated and angry. We had paid a high price for this time and I wanted more. I threw my whisky down my throat and felt it burn its way down to the knot in my stomach. Louise tried to be reassuring: 'It could be anything, Daddy, I'm sure it's nothing, probably just a swollen gland.'

We spent the weekend speculating and becoming ever more worried. I was relieved when Monday morning came around. Judy telephoned Christie and Dr Rao made an appointment to see Louise that morning. Wendy arranged for a taxi to pick up Judy and Louise. After a weekend of worrying Judy was simply too debilitated and preoccupied to drive. I stayed at home as usual.

It was a frosty bright November morning and after they had left I walked through the drifts of leaves to Poulton with Barney. He was very like Louise in so many ways and my mind was transported back to much happier days. I remember thinking that this bright little nine-year-old boy had already seen too much suffering. He loved his sister dearly and was obviously worried about this new development. In spite of everything he tried to reassure me as he bounced along kicking leaves and running ahead.

Judy telephoned at lunchtime, Louise was undergoing tests and the results wouldn't be known for a number of hours. I pictured her being poked and prodded and having those dreaded needles stuck into her yet again. As the afternoon turned to evening the tension within me became almost unbearable. What on earth would they find? Why were they taking so long? The telephone rang at almost exactly 6 p.m. It was not Judy or Louise. Dr Rao sounded tired and exasperated. The small lump was indeed malignant. I felt myself begin to tremble. Dr Rao went on to say that he had taken samples of tissue and blood which would be examined later in the week to establish if there had been any further spread. Louise would have to return to Christie the next day for a few days radiotherapy to destroy that small lump. I could hear her crying in the background. I asked Dr Rao to put her on. She had obviously been crying for some time, her voice was very hoarse.

'I'm coming home, Daddy, I'm not staying here tonight, I just want to get home.'

She began to sob quietly. What could I say? Ten months cancer free and now, it would seem, we were back to square one.

She arrived home at 7.30 p.m. looking exhausted. Her eyes were red from crying but she was smiling.

'It's only a small lump, Daddy, I'm sure they'll be able to zap it with radiotherapy.'

We spent that evening trying to make light of this sinister development; we reasoned that if Dr Rao was going to attack this small tumour with radiotherapy then there must be some hope of destroying it. In the back of my mind, though, it wasn't the small tumour that was troubling me, it was what they might find in the next few days. I braced myself in readiness for the test results.

The following morning Louise travelled to Christie by taxi. Judy was emotionally shattered and unable to face another journey and so Louise went alone. The radiotherapy only lasted for a few minutes each day and Louise was peeved that she had to stay overnight. Nan came to the rescue as usual and volunteered to go and get her one afternoon so that she could have a night at home. I remember that night quite clearly. When she got out of the car she was limping and wincing with pain. The radiotherapy had burnt her all around her groin and thigh. Yet again she had been disabled by treatment. I wondered for the thousandth time if it was all worth it. The following day the test results began to filter through. Her blood was normal; we were elated; later that day bone marrow came through – all-clear. We were ecstatic, we had one more to go. If muscle tissue was okay we would be home and dry.

Uncle Chris came round to wait for the call. I prayed, 'Please let her muscle tissue be clear; it's not a lot to ask, please God, give us this small thing.'

The telephone rang urgently, Judy answered and then came into the room.

'I don't believe it,' she said. 'She's all-clear.'

I think I leapt upon Chris. I don't think I had been so happy in my life, I wept with pure joy. There was only that small tumour and that was being attacked and destroyed. By the end of the week it was barely visible.

It was pouring with rain on that late November day. The car pulled up and Nan and Louise came through the front door. Louise was limping very badly and gingerly holding the top of her thigh: 'Fucking radiotherapy, whoever invented it should be given a dose.'

She was very badly blistered but the tumour had disappeared completely. This latest ordeal was now over, the blisters would heal – we were winning again!

The phone rang almost as soon as they sat down in the living room. It was David Cooper; he sounded a little excited.

'Philip, the Day Hospice should be nearing completion next spring and we were thinking of what we should call it. Many suggestions have been put forward, but the governing body voted unanimously for it to be named after Louise.'

I was genuinely taken aback. Many people had been involved in this huge project, not least David himself, I hadn't really thought about the possibility that they might name it after my daughter. I was thrilled, whatever happened in the future Louise was always going to have this. Louise was, of course, delighted and for a while the radiation burns were forgotten as we celebrated with Guinness and lamb curry.

By the end of November her wounds were beginning to heal. The university term was due to finish on the fourteenth of December and I had assumed that she would stay at home until after Christmas. I was mistaken. Louise couldn't wait to get back to Leeds and I really couldn't blame her. It was nearing the end of term and she had many friends to see and parties to go to.

As we drove up the approach road to Charles Morris Hall I couldn't believe my eyes. Every window of the top three floors was filled with a large letter set on coloured card. I'm sure that message could have been read by people on the other side of the city. It read Welcome Back Louise. She squealed with delight as she struggled out of the back of the car.

'We're having a party tonight,' she yelled – and they did, all night as it turned out.

A slightly hungover Louise telephoned the next day. She was free of cancer again and she was going to make the most of it.

★

The doorbell rang just as I was finishing the washing-up. It was the first week of December and we were coming to the end of what had been a memorable year. The charity was attracting lots of money, the Louise Woolcock Day Hospice was on schedule, there had been Sinead, Diana, and best of all Louise's latest tests had shown no trace of cancer. Wendy looked concerned as she sat down in the living room. I began to talk of the cancer scare of the previous month and how wonderful it was that Louise was now clear again. She stopped me in mid sentence: 'Philip,' she said, 'do you realise the significance of that scare?'

Her tone had become very serious, obviously I did not.

'Her cancer is active again, Philip,' she said.

'The other tests didn't show any trace,' I said, 'she's in the clear.'

I sat down feeling bewildered. I wanted Wendy to stop telling me things that I didn't want to hear. She had seized the moment now and she was determined to proceed.

'The tests showed no trace, but it is there somewhere,' she said, 'it will at some point reappear. Louise is not going to get better, you mustn't think otherwise.'

I had committed a cardinal error, I had dared to hope, I had stopped living one day at a time and the backward shadow of future sorrow had cast me into its shade.

On the 14 December Louise came home from Leeds as promised. She had had a wonderful term and had made some very good friends. The kitchen parties resumed with a vengeance and Louise's room was once again a hive of activity. We had her back for three whole weeks and I was living, once more, one day at a time. It was an unforgettable three weeks of shopping, laughing, drinking, talking and our fund-raising. On New Year's Eve I watched in awe as Louise stood on stage at Blackpool's Tower Ballroom and made the speech of her life in front of two thousand people. She looked so tiny and vulnerable on the huge brightly lit stage, but by the time she had finished she had the audience simultaneously reaching for both handkerchiefs and wallets. She was magnificent. We'd had a tremendous 1991 and I wondered with trepidation what 1992 might hold for us.

On the day before she was due to return to university we went for a long walk in the park. It was a grey damp January day as we walked past all our old landmarks. There was the lake where she skimmed ice in the winter and the grassy mound where we fed the ducks with my home-made inedible bread and the trees where the goblins and pixies lived. We chatted and laughed uproariously as I reminded her of her childhood. I remember thinking as she held tightly on to my arm how happy we had been and how happy we were today. Cancer could not take away our memories and it certainly wasn't having any of that day.

The next morning we packed her things (including yet another bag of oranges from Chris's mum!) and called a taxi to take her to the station. I packed a huge piece of Christmas cake and gave her some tins of Guinness. As the taxi drew away she smiled and wound down the window: 'Goodbye, King Goblin,' she shouted and then burst into laughter.

The taxi driver just shrugged his shoulders and drove away.

As usual I went to spend some time in her room. She had tidied up, but every so often I would spot something that reminded me of some evening we had enjoyed or some amusing incident. The room was by now crammed with trophies and trinkets all of which represented different stages of her cancer. Her photograph albums were bulging with memories of chemotherapy, presentation evenings, times spent with Sinead and of course that wonderful day when one princess met another.

January soon became February and following two more priceless all-clears we began, once again, to dare to hope that Wendy and Dr Rao had been wrong and that against all medical evidence Louise was going to stay cancer free for ever. We continued to take Uncle Chris over to Leeds carrying bags of oranges and distributing his largesse in the time honoured way. I loved pulling up outside the hall of residence to see her emerging from the building smiling enthusiastically. Her face always lit up when she saw Chris and he reciprocated her greeting. He was always so proud of Louise; whenever she was relating some anecdote to Judy or myself I would glance over to see Chris watching her adoringly. I have no doubt that she was the centre of his life and that the love he felt for her was immense and in many ways central to his being. At the end of each visit we would stand on those huge steps trying to prolong the moment. But as Chris produced his twenty pound note we knew it was time to say goodbye.

'Whatever you do don't spend it on anything sensible,' Chris always said, and Louise never let him down.

It was mid-February 1992 when the local newspaper telephoned. We had by now become well used to calls from the *Evening Gazette* enquiring as to the state of the fund or of Louise. They had been tremendously supportive and one or two of their reporters had become good friends. This time though it was the editor.

'Philip did you know that Diana is coming back to Blackpool to open Louise's day hospice?'

I was incredulous. I had written to her as requested but had heard nothing and assumed that we had not been lucky this time. Then I remembered the look she had given me, 'Write to me, Philip,' she had said.

There had definitely been something in her tone that day. I was overjoyed we were going to see her again in five months time. On 28 July, 1992 the Princess of Wales was going to travel north to open our day hospice. Better still, Louise was still well, just five more all-clears and we'd be home and dry. I phoned Louise at

Leeds and spoke to the college warden. As I left the message with her she sounded both delighted and a little conspiratorial.

'You bastard, Daddy!' Louise said excited and happy, 'you bloody bastard. I've just been pulled by the fucking warden.' She started to laugh. 'I didn't know what it was about, she was so bloody serious, I just got this message to say I had to see the warden and then she started to talk as if I was in trouble. I thought I'd been grassed up for blowing up the landing's electric kettle.'

The warden had decided to enjoy herself at Louise's expense. She had adopted a serious tone and Louise had been convinced that some misdemeanour had been uncovered. Louise was about to confess to the destruction of the kettle when the warden had let go the ruse and told Louise that her father had phoned and Diana was coming up to open her day hospice in July. At this point the warden had embraced Louise and proceeded to dance her around her office in celebration. Of course Louise had joined her enthusiastically as much in relief as delight! But there was no doubt that she was delighted.

'Twice, Daddy, twice. I can't wait to see her again, I knew she'd come back.'

Chapter Six

Easter of 1992 was to be a significant turning point in Louise's remarkable odyssey. She came home for the holiday and as she got out of her taxi I noticed that she wasn't moving properly. She seemed to struggle and have difficulty getting out of the seat. I went out to get her luggage from the boot and noticed that she was breathing heavily and looking distressed.

'Fucking ten pin bowling, I've strained my bloody back, I knew I shouldn't have gone.'

I felt immediately relieved. She had pulled a muscle, no problem. I gave her two paracetemol and by bedtime she was fine. The next morning she was back to normal sitting chatting on the end of the bed about her superb end of term exam results, and making plans for seeing friends in town later that day. Kitchen parties resumed and arrangements were made for Diana's next visit. Life at that time could not have been much better.

It was about halfway through that holiday that Louise began to play 'cat and mouse'. I remember the day well. I took my car to be serviced and asked Louise if she would stay at home and look after her nine-year-old brother until we returned. She had reluctantly agreed but she was in a very tetchy mood that day. We dropped the car at the garage and decided to walk the three miles home. It was a beautiful day and Louise had, quite frankly, been getting on my nerves. I telephoned her about half a mile from home to see how things were.

'You'd better get home now or I'll kill this little sod,' she shouted.

She sounded furious and I wondered just what Barney could have done to make her so angry.

When we arrived home her mood had worsened. It was true that Barney had been a little naughty, but no more than any normal nine-year-old. She loved her youngest brother deeply and was normally very tolerant of his excesses. She began to rant about the unfairness of having been asked to look after him. I could feel her temper rising, and for the first time I turned on her: 'You self-centred little sod, we never ask you for anything; we've all been through this cancer, we've all suffered with you.'

I could feel myself losing control and it felt cathartic, I hadn't expressed so much anger for years. She looked shocked and hurt. For a moment I thought she might retaliate. I was shaking with anger; I had lived with tension for too long and the dam had finally burst. Her eyes began to fill with tears.

'I can't help it, this bloody pain in my back is driving me mad.'

For two weeks this cat and mouse game had proceeded – 'the pain is here and then it's not and then it's back again' – I could take no more. I told her that she should return to Christie and the tears flowed.

'I'm not going back to that fucking charnel house, I just want to be left alone,' she said. 'I can't take any more, I just can't take any more of this fucking torture, Daddy, I want my life back now.'

She couldn't speak, emotion had taken over from reason. She fled to her room and sanctuary.

That night I telephoned the hospice. I needed some sort of reassurance that my shouting at her was in some way justifiable. I felt horrible, I had behaved in a selfish and cruel way. I spoke to a senior nurse and found myself seeking chastisement for my cruelty to her. I was tired and confused and completely at this nurse's mercy. She was calm and reassuring. She told me that I had needed to release that anger and that Louise would under-stand that the anger was not directed at her but at this whole impossibly painful situation. She talked about how much she admired us as a family and that our coping strategies were both necessary and appropriate. In the end she neither chastised nor attempted to justify my attack on Louise. She simply confirmed that it was necessary. We spoke for an hour and at the end of that time I felt reassured, my guilt had been expertly assuaged, but more importantly I felt needed once again.

I put down the receiver and went to Louise's room. She was fast asleep and had not drawn the curtains. I quietly sat on the end of her bed. Her room was lit by a bright silver full moon, everything was perfectly still. She looked serene and ageless in that moment of beautiful tranquillity. She must have sensed my presence as she slept for she opened her eyes and tried to smile.

'Are you all right, Daddy?' she whispered, and then she drifted back to her painless world of dreams.

The next morning she had difficulty getting out of bed and we called our GP. After a cursory examination he prescribed some strong painkillers. Two hours later Louise was up and about but soon her pain had returned. I telephoned Dr Rao at Christie but he didn't seem too concerned. He explained that the radiotherapy she had had six months before was probably responsible for her back pain. He suggested that she should travel to Christie the next day and he would treat her by administering a mild dose of radiotherapy to her painful back. He assured me that after a few sessions of treatment her pain would ease. I was puzzled. If radiotherapy had caused this then how could it cure it? Nonetheless I was happy to go along with his suggestion. I had no reason to doubt this man who had become so central to our lives and Louise's future.

The back pain by now had become so severe that painkillers were rendered useless and Louise was left with no option but to return to Christie. This time though she was insistent that she would not stay overnight but return each evening to her sanctuary. And so it was arranged that Judy would take her and bring her home again every day so she could be given yet more radiotherapy for this awful pain. Dr Rao was right, the pain went away almost immediately, and following a few sessions she was pronounced fit to return to her other life in Leeds.

And so in early May 1992 she returned to that other place where life was lived at a different pace and in a very different way; a place where Louise was able to shed the mantle of cancer and join a somewhat different world. Once again the phone calls started, pubs were revisited and exams studied for. She sat those first year exams towards the end of that month and came ahead of her whole year. She was awarded one hundred per cent in German linguistics. Such a mark had not been awarded by the university for twenty years. She was thrilled as she told me about it. I thought about her teachers in primary school, and I felt unforgivably smug!

Very shortly after her exam success she came home for a long weekend. Ostensibly it was to see her friend Steven and to shop for clothes for the university summer ball. But as she climbed out of the taxi on that hot June morning I knew something was wrong. She looked ghastly pale and her eyes were sunken and tired. Moreover, she was obviously in pain again and winced as she lifted her hand luggage. I asked her if she was okay and she told me she was fine.

She could never lie convincingly and as I made her a cup of tea in the kitchen she tried to sound enthusiastic about the end of term functions to which she had been invited. I pretended to be interested but my thoughts were elsewhere. As she picked up her cup I noticed that her hand was trembling slightly and she seemed to have lost some weight. At lunchtime we walked up to the pub for a drink with Uncle Chris. Normally the prospect of seeing Chris caused Louise to become animated and chatty. Today, however, was different, she seemed too quiet, and as she walked alongside me in the hot summer sun, she seemed preoccupied and also a little breathless. Chris enquired enthusiastically about Leeds but Louise's responses were not full of her usual fervour. No amusing anecdotes were forthcoming and she sat looking thoughtfully at her glass of diet coke.

When we got home she went to her room and before long I sensed that she had fallen asleep. About two hours later she struggled downstairs gasping for breath and with her eyes full of tears.

'The pain in my back has come back, Daddy. I'm not going back to Christie, I've been through enough.'

I wasn't shocked, I knew that things weren't right and I knew in my heart that we were entering the final lap of this extraordinary marathon. I told Louise gently but firmly that we had no choice; that I was sure that there was nothing drastically wrong and that Dr Rao would, as always, have all the answers. Of course, I was completely unconvincing. I felt hollow and emotionally adrift. Louise looked at me with her brimming eyes.

'Don't worry, Daddy,' she said, 'I'll be okay.'

That weekend is almost completely wiped from my memory. I

recall that Louise's friend Steven visited and that he brought an Italian friend from university who spent the Sunday night in our spare room. I can remember clearly, however, that Monday morning in early June. I walked into the living room and Louise was sitting in an easy chair whilst Gianna Luca, Steven's friend, was busy kneeling at her feet lacing up her Doc Martens. The ambulance was due to take her to Christie for tests, and as I watched this young man lacing up Louise's boots I noticed that the pink had gone from her cheeks and the light had left her eyes completely. But mostly I remember that she looked ever so slightly pale yellow, and she seemed very thoughtful.

Almost as soon as Judy left with her in the ambulance the doorbell rang. Father Fred was looking concerned.

'Pheel! I saw the ambulance, is Louise okay?'

During the preceding six months Fred Okai had become very important to us all. He had been in England for about twelve months and was working as a Priest at St John's Catholic Church in Poulton. He had originally befriended our next door neighbour, who was a devout catholic, and she had introduced him to me. I have to say that I didn't go so much on priests, but Fred was different. He was a small man from Ghana with a huge flashing smile, an electrifying presence and a sharp intelligence. He was hugely compassionate, not in a patronising way but challenging and completely unorthodox. I suppose that if the Catholic Church had a libertarian conscience then he was it. We had spent many long hours arguing about theology, philosophy and even politics, and I honestly don't think I ever got the better of him. Fred was devoid of malice and full of love, especially for Louise. He adored my daughter and always seemed to appear during a crisis like all the best guardian angels. That morning I could not have been more pleased to see him.

I explained to Fred that Louise's pain had returned and that she had gone to Christie for tests to see what was going on. I told him that I feared the worst. He told me that whatever the outcome Louise was an incredible young woman and would cope with anything fate had to throw at her.

'There is some purpose to all of this, Pheel,' he said as if contemplating something distant and untouchable. 'Louise is very special, she is exceptional.' He became thoughtful again and then became serious as he fixed my eye. 'I will be here, Pheel, I am your brother.'

I smiled, I was white, six feet two inches tall from the suburban north of England. Fred was jet black, five feet three inches from rural Ghana. And yet he was right, this bond between us was to prove priceless; and to this day, I believe, heaven sent.

It was probably about lunchtime when the telephone rang and I was still thinking about what Fred had said. It was Judy.

'They've told Louise.' Her voice was numb and distant. 'She's got a huge tumour in her pelvis.'

I could hear Louise in the background as Dr Rao took the telephone. 'I'm so sorry Philip,' he was close to tears, 'we've done everything that we can, it's just a matter of time now.'

Suddenly Louise was on the phone sobbing. 'No, Daddy, no, I can't die,' she could hardly control her breathing 'I'm too young, Daddy, I've got too much to do, Daddy, tell them please tell them.'

I asked her to put Dr Rao back on.

'How much time?' I asked.

I was on automatic pilot, it was no longer me talking. I was shaken beyond tears now. My daughter was pleading for me to save her and I felt helpless, useless and hopeless.

'It's hard to say, Philip, six months maybe, possibly twelve, we've told Louise.'

I heard her in the background screaming now. 'You know what you can do with your fucking six months.'

Judy came back on the phone to tell me that the ambulance would be setting off back in a few minutes, there was no life left in her voice. Like me, she was somewhere else.

I put down the telephone and walked blindly to Louise's room. I sat down on her bed. It was unmade and her pink dressing gown was strewn across it. I picked it up and stared through my tears.

'What larks Louise,' I said, 'what larks.' I spoke as if she were there with me. 'What are we going to do now?'

The room seemed to take on a new significance now. The story of that tremendous journey was all around me: pictures of Diana, Sinead, Germany, the kitchen parties. Photos of our

85

charity work, letters of thanks and of support. But more important than all of these were the personal and private memories of our battle together. The vicious chemotherapy, the God given remission and those timeless moments spent together during extremes of happiness and harsh adversity. I could almost feel her spirit now. I tried to picture her returning to me pale, shaking and confused. How would she cope with her death sentence? She was just twenty-one. Bright, pretty and eccentric, an incredible courageous spirit. She had brought so much light to all our lives and I feared that when that light finally went out there would be nothing worth having in my life. I couldn't contemplate life without her, she had become my life. I shuddered and tried to put these thoughts out of my mind. 'One day at a time, Philip, she's on her way home, she needs you more than ever, don't go under now, you owe her more than that.'

The doorbell rang and for a moment I thought I might have been dreaming. The man from the hospice explained that he had been sent to deliver a large Parker Knoll recliner chair. I had completely forgotten that I had spoken to David Cooper some days previously and that he had offered us the loan of this chair to help ease Louise's back pain. We struggled to get this huge and hideous green chair into our pink living room. When he had gone I just stood looking at this garish intruder wondering where on earth it could go. I looked around in exasperation and decided it should stay just where it was, in the middle of the room and there it sat like some great dark green toad, a horrible reminder of our awful situation.

I heard the ambulance outside and my stomach tightened. I had no idea as to what state Louise would be in. How was a young woman to respond to such news? Would she be calmer now or still hysterical? She walked into the living room followed by Judy. Louise's face was tear-streaked and her eyes were red and sore. She hardly seemed to notice the chair as she put her arms around my waist.

'Oh, Daddy, I feel terrible, what are we going to do?'

There was no answer to this question, nor did she expect one. We were both terrified. The battle was finally over and time had become both an ally and a powerful enemy.

She sank into the great green chair and I lifted the foot-rest for her. Nan arrived looking shocked, her eyes were brimming with tears. As she knelt beside the chair Louise began to sob quietly.

'Oh, Nan, I'm scared, I'm going to die and there's nothing I can do about it.' Nan didn't reply. Like me she realised that there was nothing that she could say.

I went into the kitchen with Judy. I could sense that she had more to tell. Dr Rao had indeed taken her to one side, as I had feared. Louise did have a tumour in her pelvis and that was responsible for the back pain. Dr Rao had known that this was the case some weeks before but for some reason he decided not to tell us. He had zapped it with radiotherapy to allow Louise one last trip to Germany and in the vain hope that she could complete her first year at Leeds. The prognosis for Louise was more awful than I had dared to imagine. The tumour was likely to twist its way up her spine causing paralysis, and then to her brain causing blindness and death. Louise would suffer a good deal of nausea and pain in the interim. Cancer had taken hold and it was going to demonstrate the whole array of its talents and show us every facet of its hideous face before it finally took her away.

I began to give this cancer a human dimension. I visualised it as the personification of evil, lurking and smiling with smug satisfaction as it waited to claim this beautiful young woman. It was then that I became firmly convinced that it could not win, for it would die with her. It could never touch her incredible spirit nor sully her beauty. I felt satisfied and comfortable with these thoughts and I began to feel a great strength well up from within. I had dug deep and I was not going to be found wanting. We would fight this together and, although she would die, we would win.

When I returned to the living room Louise was sitting in her green chair. Her eyes were becoming heavy with sleep and she asked me to help her to her room. She lay on her bed and I held her hand.

'I'm going to have a sleep now, Daddy, I'm really tired.' She closed her eyes, 'What larks, Daddy, what larks, just think only another five years. Dr Rao says I've only got another five years. Maybe they'll have found a cure by then.'

With this strange pronouncement she drifted off to sleep. I went downstairs.

'Judy, she's talking about five years,' I said.

Judy confirmed that on the way home in the ambulance Louise had had a similar conversation with her. For some reason she had decided that Dr Rao had given her five years to live. His realistic prognosis of six to twelve months had been filed away somewhere in the deepest recesses of her mind. Five years had become her way of coping, the truth had simply failed to register, and I was glad.

I telephoned Uncle Chris. He immediately went into denial.

'Bollocks, they don't know what they're talking about.' He hesitated for a few seconds. 'Anyway, why did they tell her, the stupid bastards.'

His voice was full of anger and pain. He has always refused to accept the fact that Louise might die, in spite of all the medical evidence to this effect. And so every person who was close to Louise brought different coping strategies into play until finally I spoke to Father Fred.

'Oh, Pheel, you must be strong, she needs you more than ever now. You will find the strength, God will be there when you need him. He will not abandon you.'

There was certainty in Fred's voice and he was smiling, but his eyes were full of tears.

The vomiting started a few days afterwards. We didn't know exactly why but Dr Rao thought that the cancer had probably spread to her stomach. It was rampant now, no treatment in the world could have slowed its progress. A few days later I found her sitting on the edge of her bed crying.

'Daddy, I can't stand up. I can't bloody well stand up, my legs won't work properly.'

I put my arm around her thin shoulders and thought that it was all happening too quickly. I gave her a squeeze and she cried out in pain. There were tumours under her arm and in her shoulder. I gave her a spoonful of liquid morphine to ease the pain and Judy phoned Dr Rao.

The ambulance arrived within an hour. Dr Rao decided to zap her shoulder and armpit with radiotherapy to shrink these painful growths. When she had gone Fred called and we talked for two or three hours as I tried to make sense of everything. His role as my spiritual mentor had become pivotal to everything that I thought and did. There were also practical considerations. The university were, of course, aware that Louise's cancer was no longer in remission, but no arrangements had been made to empty her room and return her belongings to Poulton. It had been bad enough watching her tearfully come to terms with the fact that she could never return to live in her much loved Leeds, but harsh reality was going to hit home as arrangements had to be made for the posters, rugs and other precious items of memorabilia to be transported back across the Pennines. Bringing back all of those wonderful memories was going to be a heartbreaking task.

It was mid-June 1992 when I phoned the university. Louise's condition was by now so advanced that she couldn't walk any distance unaided. She was losing weight and her cheeks had taken on a sunken appearance. Her deterioration had been rapid. Greg Benton was a lecturer in Chinese Studies and the warden of Louise's hall of residence. He had been responsible for discipline within the Hall and this had occasionally brought him into conflict with Louise who had been the Students representative. I explained to Dr Benton that we needed to move Louise's belongings back to Poulton, and proceeded to ask him when we might conveniently drive over to Leeds to get this awful task over with.

'I'll drive her stuff over to Poulton, Philip, would this Sunday suit?'

I protested weakly that it would take the best part of a day to pack and drive over and then return to Leeds.

'That's no problem, but if you could organise lunch I'd be ever so grateful.'

I didn't realise at the time but in spite of their necessarily adversarial positions Greg Benton had become a Louise fan; a mutual respect had developed, and it turned out that there was little or nothing he wouldn't do for her.

The emphasis of caring for Louise was rapidly switching to pain control. Morphine was wonderful, but it caused her to sleep a lot, and when she wasn't asleep she was often very drowsy.

Some days were better than others. On some days she could walk almost unaided, on others she needed a wheelchair. Some days she couldn't bear to be touched because of joint pain and on others her pain was controllable. The nausea too came and went. One small meal would stay down, the next would return immediately almost intact.

On that bright Sunday in late June she was having one of her better days when Greg Benton's tiny, and rather shabby, old Fiat pulled up outside the house. It looked quite comical with Louise's possessions piled in the back and lashed untidily to the roof. Dr Benton was a middle aged academic. He was a highly rated teacher with a reputation for mild eccentricity, harsh discipline and a love of whisky. He got out of the car and I went out to greet him. His car was followed by another containing some of Louise's friends from university. The plan was that I would keep Louise occupied downstairs whilst Judy unloaded her possessions and tried to recreate the feel of her room in Leeds in her bedroom at home. We had decided that it would be too upsetting for her to see her things being unpacked and simply piled into her room.

I ushered Greg Benton through to the dining room and shouted upstairs for Louise to come from her room. I poured him a glass of whisky and as he sat down at the table I heard Louise struggling downstairs. She was breathing heavily and cursing with each step. Dr Benton looked troubled as he heard her approach along the hallway. When she finally entered the room he looked shocked. She had probably been away from university for only three or four weeks but in that short time her physical appearance must have changed more than I had thought.

Greg Benton was hugely attentive and immediately all formalities between warden and student were dropped. We must have talked for over an hour. He was fascinated as Louise and I talked of the past. He was spellbound by stories of pixies and goblins and of Louise's difficult school life. I watched him as she charmed him mercilessly. He told us how he had been drawn to Louise from the beginning of her time at Leeds. He spoke affectionately of her eccentricity, her strength of character, of their arguments and of just how much Louise had brought to his hall of residence. He spoke in detail of one night when he had (goodness knows how) dropped all his keys out of the window of his flat in the early hours of the morning. The keys had landed on Louise's window sill two or three floors below. For some months before Dr Benton had been waging war upon Louise and her friends over their nocturnal parties and associated noise. He related with good humoured embarrassment how at 2 a.m. he had been forced to knock on Louise's door to retrieve his keys, only to be given a lecture on the lack of consideration involved in waking people up during the early hours of the morning. This lecture was delivered in front of a large number of students who had been (deliberately) awoken by the sound of Louise's voice and who, Dr Benton related, were taking great enjoyment in seeing their hall warden being soundly ticked off for creeping about disturbing people at such an unearthly hour! It was obvious that Greg Benton considered Louise to be a worthy opponent, and equally obvious, from his stories, that they had crossed swords on more than one occasion.

It was a wonderful afternoon. Greg Benton's fascination with Louise grew by the hour. He insisted that she took him to her room and over a long period they sat on her bed together whilst he inspected her photos. He seemed particularly interested in the much younger child and just how she came to be who she was. Louise, for her part was equally fascinated by the fact that her erstwhile enemy, the austere and somewhat distant figure of authority, the warden of Charles Morris Hall, was now lounging on her bed laughing uproariously as she related stories of her childhood. Meanwhile, the other students had been watching in awe as their tutor metamorphosed from hall warden to real human being in front of their very eyes. One young man, a student of Chinese, who had held Dr Benton in the greatest awe and who had from time to time been the subject of his ire, was so taken aback at being allowed to call him Greg, had spent the whole afternoon in rapturous delight using that name as often as possible.

'Greg, would you like some more wine? Are you going on holiday this year Greg? Has Greg got enough potatoes?'

And so it went, for the whole afternoon. Every time that poor young man said the word *Greg*, Louise and Annette collapsed in fits of hysterical laughter.

Strangely, during that tremendous afternoon Louise never once vomited nor did she complain of any pain. It was a sad moment when the party had to end. Even sadder for the wretched young man who had enjoyed so much the freedom of being allowed to call his senior tutor by his first name for such a long time, and would now have to revert to Dr Benton. Poor 'Briefly' (so called because he carried a briefcase everywhere, even to bed, it was rumoured!) had been struggling with ancient Mandarin and Greg Benton had been making his life a misery. He must have hoped, as he replenished Greg's glass or earnestly sought Greg's opinion, that it would be forever Greg. Alas it was not to be and I heard that Greg soon metamorphosed back into Dr Benton upon their return to college.

Louise had hoped against hope that she would be able to attend the university summer ball the following week. Her friend Steven had bought tickets some weeks before, but as her illness progressed so her chances of going seemed to disappear. She desperately wanted one last chance to see her friends. They had been travelling over from Leeds in two's and three's to see her since her illness had returned. But Louise's heart was set on attending that Ball.

Shortly after Greg Benton left Louise announced that she would, like Cinderella, be going to the ball. Greg had told her that he would be going away for the last week in June and that he would leave the keys to his flat with the college bursar. If Louise was well enough she could use his flat to stay over in Leeds and attend the summer ball. She was thrilled. Two clear targets now lay not too far ahead. In the next few weeks she would go to the Ball and she would meet her Princess for the second time.

At the end of a June in which her health had deteriorated ever more, Judy drove her over to Leeds with Steven. It was, of course, to be her last trip and she knew it. She approached it with typical gutsy determination. She bought a beautiful sparkling dress and spent a fabulous weekend with Steven in Dr Benton's huge, but rather bare flat. She returned tired but very happy. She related stories of drinking and behaviour of an immeasurably bad kind – all, of course, undertaken by others. She talked of the contents of the infamous Dr Benton's fridge and wondered out loud just why he kept only a half bottle of scotch in there! As she lay on her bed talking quietly between laboured breaths, I noticed that blood was staining her dry, cracked lips. Another symptom was making its terrible presence felt. Her gums had begun to bleed and her yellow tinged face gave her the appearance of a Halloween mask.

Chapter Seven

The doorbell rang early the next morning, it was David Cooper. He went to Louise's room to sit with her for a while. We had been up for most of the previous night listening to her pitiful cries as she tried to sleep between morphine induced hallucinations. David came downstairs and into the kitchen, he looked preoccupied.

'Tell me honestly, Philip, how long do you think she can go on like this?'

I was high on exhaustion and his voice seemed like a distant echo. The seriousness of his question didn't register properly.

'How do I know?' I said. 'Six, maybe seven weeks?' I thought for a minute. 'I just wish we could take her somewhere – do something together before she dies.'

I noticed that my face was wet with tears but I wasn't crying. I didn't want to contemplate her death. I wanted to continue living one day at a time, I wanted David to go away but he stood his ground.

'I've just been talking to Louise about getting away for a few days, together as a family, a sort of last holiday. You're all shattered, you can't carry on like this. We can keep Louise going with morphine and steroids. You could probably manage three or four days away, what do you think?'

I told David that it would be impossible. 'She vomits all the time, some days her pain is so great she can hardly sit down, how the hell can we go anywhere?'

'Louise wants to go Penzance in Cornwall, and I think she can make it.'

Penzance was a nine hour non-stop drive from our town and I laughed bitterly as David continued in earnest.

'Keith Gledhill will lend us his light aircraft, you can be there in an hour and a half.'

It was true that Louise had talked of visiting south-west Cornwall. All my relatives on my father's side had come from the Lizard Peninsula. As he had got older my father began talking of his roots and his desire to return to his homeland. I was puzzled nonetheless by Louise's strange request and felt determined to find out why, when offered access to the whole British mainland, she had chosen this remote place.

'I don't know, Daddy, we'll see,' she said and smiled enigmatically as she wiped the blood from around her mouth.

Monday 6 July, 1992 was oppressively hot and also sunny. It was important that we had a cloudless day for we were flying from the Lancashire coast across Wales to the south-west peninsular of England, and at a height of nine thousand feet the view would be tremendous. I had persuaded Mick Smithson to pick us up in his brand new Bentley to take us to the local airport for 9 a.m. Mick was a local businessman and drinking partner; he hadn't taken much persuading, for like Dr Benton he had some years before come under Louise's spell. I wanted this to be a special day in every sense and so at 8.30 a.m. the Bentley pulled up outside the house. So much was reminiscent of the year before when we had all set off to meet Diana for the first time, except that then Louise was in remission, and today Judy was sitting with her on her bed holding her sick bowl whilst she regurgitated the meagre breakfast she had consumed not thirty minutes before. She struggled downstairs as we both held on to her arms and led her to the safety of each stair. She was shaking with weakness and totally emaciated, but as we moved her laboriously towards the front door she sounded determined.

'I will go to Cornwall no matter what; this bastard has had its say today, now it can fuck off, I'm on my way!'

We manoeuvred her into the white leather rear of the car and I got into the front. Mick checked his mirror and pulled away.

It was only five miles to Squires Gate Airport and after a few minutes Louise seemed settled. Sam and Barney were chatting excitedly on either side of her and Judy. We were going to fly to Royal Naval Air Station Culdrose and the Royal Navy were going to arrange for a minibus to take us on the few miles to Penzance and the Queens Hotel where David had booked our rooms. As we approached the airport Louise began to retch and curse, as Judy grabbed the sick bowl I glanced at Mick. He was watching her in the mirror and he flinched with pain and anger at the injustice of it all.

'I'm so sorry, Phil, I'm just so sorry, it's not bloody right,' he said as he pulled alongside the aircraft.

We manhandled her gently from the back of the car. Every so often she cried out in pain. As Mick held hold of her arm his face changed from great concern to out and out horror as he realised that most of her flesh had been consumed by this parasitic cancer.

'There's almost nothing left of her, Phil,' he said and his bottom lip began to give way. I took over.

We helped Louise into the small aircraft each of us taking hold of a boot, a hand or an elbow. I noticed her brothers puffing and panting determinedly, taking over from adults and reassuring them in their embarrassment as Louise whimpered with pain. They were growing up quickly and I felt both proud and sad. By the time we had filled this tiny six seater plane with our luggage and taken our seats Louise was trembling with exhaustion and I with fear. I had been dreading this flight for days now and had made no secret of my intense and very real fear. Proper aeroplanes made me into a gibbering wreck, and as we took off my family always gave me disgusted glances (and worse) as I reached out a sweaty hand to whoever had the misfortune of sitting next to me, in the vain hope that they might offer some reassurance.

This was much worse, though. This plane seemed to be made of balsa wood and glue! As the pilot began to taxi towards the runway I began to shake and mutter incoherently, my palms began to sweat and my breathing became mechanical, like a life support machine. Sam, Barney and Judy began to laugh and, as I retorted angrily in frustration and sheer terror, a thin hand reached across and held mine tightly.

'Are you all right, Daddy,' she said and I felt foolish and ashamed. She was sitting opposite me, and in spite of the heat was wrapped in a thick blanket and shivering. 'You'll be okay, Daddy, just hold on to me, don't worry.'

And so in terror I held on to her broken body until my fear subsided, encouraged all the while by her gentle reassurance and love. An angel of mercy in the clutches of death.

The Navy couldn't have been more helpful. They assiduously attended to Louise's every need. But their faces said so much. One officer brought her a glass of orange juice on to the tarmac and I watched her as she watched Louise trying to swallow. I knew this young woman must have felt useless, and worse, helpless. She kept looking at me as if to say, 'This is too horrible, please let me help.'

I smiled at her, 'It's okay,' I said, 'we're fine.'

She was close to tears and I think my reassurance made things worse; she turned quickly away and walked towards another female officer. A minute later I noticed the poor woman being helped away by her colleague towards the terminal building. The close proximity of suffering was too much for her.

Those few days in Cornwall were to prove strange indeed. The rest of that first day was memorable in that Louise was relatively well. She actually ate a jacket potato and prawn salad and was not sick; this certainly counted as memorable. Of course, we were thrilled, but during the first night cancer returned with a vengeance. We didn't sleep much as Louise's cries of pain became more desperate, so we became more exhausted. Every so often she cried out and we responded with morphine and love, and yet more morphine and by each morning we were emotionally finished beyond tiredness and sometimes beyond caring any more. But two things stand out about that time in Cornwall, and I am still convinced that we went there for a purpose.

On the second day of our four days away Judy came from Louise's room at about 8 a.m., she looked shattered and had obviously not slept for some hours.

'It's your turn now,' she said, 'I've really got to get some sleep.'

We had been taking it in turns to nurse Louise and alternately try to look after Sam and Barney. It was murder and the holiday was rapidly becoming something of a nightmare as we tried to balance the needs of the boys against the demands that Louise was now making. I walked into Louise's room fully expecting to be measuring yet another dose of morphine. She was sitting on her bed fully dressed in jeans and Doc Martens. It had been a difficult night, but in spite of her haggard and drawn appearance I noticed that some brightness had returned to her eyes.

'Let's go for a walk, Daddy, it's a beautiful day.'

I was taken aback at first. She had been so dreadfully incapacitated of late and my first thought was that I was dreaming all this; that this was an illusion brought about by exhaustion. Nonetheless, I went along with her request. I put up her wheelchair and lifted her into it with great ease. There were no cries of pain and I decided to ride my luck taking the lift down to the ground floor. We were soon outside in the bright warm sunshine and I asked Louise which way we should go.

'There, Daddy,' she said and pointed firmly towards the hamlet of Newlyn about a mile along the coast. 'We're going there, Daddy.'

I knelt beside her to adjust the brakes on her chair and noticed that she was smiling contentedly, all the lines of pain had left her face and she had somehow come back to life again.

'Come on, Daddy I want to take some photographs, it's a gorgeous day let's go and have some larks.'

It was indeed a perfect summer morning as I wheeled her along the deserted sea front. The sun was hot on our backs and the blue surf sparkled and hissed as it gently lapped the sand and gravel.

'I'm going to enjoy this time, Daddy, we'll get some postcards and go to a pub; yes, Daddy, let's go and have a drink.'

'You'll be sick, Louise; look, you're feeling better today let's not spoil it.'

I tried to dissuade her but she was adamant. I had not heard her sounding so happy for months, she chattered without a break for the duration of our walk. She made jokes and talked of the past. She reminisced about fairies and goblins and of the magical times. She was transformed that morning and I was with her again completely; I could feel myself being drawn in as her spirit seemed to leave her ravaged body and seduce me to become part of her once more.

It was as if by magic that she directed me up a cobbled side street in this small fishing village.

'Come along, Daddy, push me up here, this looks interesting.'

It was almost as if she had been there before. It didn't look at all interesting, but at the end of this tiny street there was a quaint little pub that had opened far too early, and at the side was a tiny garden with a view of Newlyn harbour.

'Here, Daddy, we'll sit here in the garden and we'll drink cider.'

I protested that we had forgotten the sick bowls and that her mother would be furious if I made her ill. She ignored me.

'I'll have a half and you can have a pint. Anyway, how can you make me ill?' she laughed and I did as I was bid.

There followed a most peaceful and tranquil hour as we sat together in the hot sun drinking our cider and just being together. Louise became very pensive from time to time as she stared across the little harbour.

'It's been strange, Daddy.'

'What has Louise?'

'You know, everything that has happened to us.'

'How do you mean, Louise?'

'Well, it was all so unexpected, we couldn't have prepared for any of this, and yet sometimes we've been so happy. It's been special hasn't it, Daddy?' I looked at her, she was deep in thought. 'I'm glad we're not a normal family,' she said. She reached over and laid her bloodless white hand on my forearm. 'I don't think a normal family could have coped with all this.'

She smiled and for the thousandth time I felt like an uncomprehending five-year-old who hadn't quite grasped everything but knew that something significant was going on.

'We've had some larks, Louise.'

She smiled again.

'More than that, Daddy, we've had so much more than that.'

She rolled her wheelchair slowly towards me. She put her arms around my neck and I felt her fleshless cheekbone press into the side of my face. She smelt of cider.

'Oh, Daddy, I wish we could stay like this for ever, together in this place. I don't need morphine, I feel happy now.'

I could feel her heart beating faintly and my thoughts raced horribly towards the inevitable end. I also wanted this moment to last for ever and I prayed that there would be life after death, for I felt that this was as close to paradise as I could ever get on earth. To spend eternity with Louise in all our favourite places during all the enchanting seasons at all stages of her short life. To have all our special times rolled into one for ever – that would indeed be heaven.

During that hour together we had said so much with so few words. Our spirits had become as one. It was as if cancer had never made its vile presence felt. We had shared some moments of great joy and beauty together, and like all true beauty it had to end. But I knew the memory of that magical time would live for ever. As I wheeled her back along the sea front I thanked God for that time, for it was most certainly God given. The very fact that she had been able to drink a half pint of cider without vomiting was a miracle in itself. Her energy had returned as had the light in her eyes, and most important, her wonderful and beautiful spirit had seduced me completely. When we finally returned to our hotel I felt spiritually and emotionally refreshed. We had enjoyed our last drink together.

*

The owner of the Queens Hotel, Sheila Hicks, was a lovely woman in late middle age who had recently lost her much loved husband. Within an hour of our arrival she had befriended Louise, and Louise had reciprocated that genuine friendship. Sheila had a daughter who lived in a small village called St Just, a few miles from Penzance. My father's family had originally come from St Just and so I was thrilled when Sheila's daughter invited us to her house for lunch the day before we were due to leave for home.

After a delightful lunch Louise became tired and needed to lie down. We made her comfortable on a huge sofa and gave her morphine for her pain. We wrapped her in a blanket and soon she fell into a deep sleep. It was a pleasant, if overcast, afternoon and we were grateful for the chance to leave Louise in safe hands whilst we went for a walk.

As we climbed the steep winding hill out of St Just I felt a strong sense of purpose, of being led to something important. It was almost like a sense of destiny; I knew I was going to find something. Before too long we found ourselves in a large windswept graveyard and strongly drawn towards one part of it. The next thing I remember was reading the inscription, *I will swallow up death in victory and the Lord God shall wipe away the tears from their eyes.* Somehow I had found myself beside my grandfather's grave. I felt a huge jolt of raw emotion and disbelief. And those words, those words said it all.

My grandfather had always been a larger than life figure. He was a miner and a drinking man who had had a certain reputation within this incestuous Methodist community in south-west Cornwall. He had emigrated to South Dakota where he had used his raw talent to become a US Marshall and Chief of Police in Lead City at a time when outlaws were legendary. I had seen newspaper cuttings of his exploits, and as a young child, I had handled his huge Smith and Wesson revolver and worn his Marshall's badge with great pride. I looked once more in utter bewilderment at this ornate weather worn piece of Cornish granite and knew from deep within my heart that Louise had brought me here for a reason. I read the inscription again and began to cry. 'I will swallow up death in victory…' at that moment everything seemed to have a very strong purpose and meaning. Louise had only vaguely been aware of my grandfather's existence, and for my part I believed he had died and been buried in the USA; yet strangely from deep within his forgotten grave my grandfather had offered me words of great comfort. We returned to the house, Louise had been in a deep sleep. She stirred sleepily as we entered the room.

'I've just had a beautiful dream, Daddy, are you okay?'

★

We returned home to Poulton after a very disturbed last night in Cornwall. During the night pain control had become all but impossible and morphine was causing Louise to hallucinate horribly. In the end we had to call out a local GP in the middle of the night. I remember sitting in the half light of Louise's hotel room whilst this poor woman examined Louise and expressed great concern about whether she would be well enough to fly home the following day. She also expressed great concern for Judy and myself. Louise's illness was by now leaving us emotionally fraught – we had been living on adrenaline for just too long.

As we pulled up outside the house David Cooper's car pulled up behind us. He followed us inside looking concerned. Louise collapsed into the green chair and I sat on the sofa. David knelt at Louise's feet looking at her intently.

'Philip would you mind making us a cup of tea?'

At first I didn't take the hint.

'For Christ's sake, just a minute, David, I'm knackered!'

He looked at me and gestured with his eyes for me to leave. I went into the kitchen and drew hard on my cigarette. As the nicotine hit the spot I felt my body pull back from the brink of complete exhaustion. I looked at the pile of luggage in the hall and thought about events of the last few days. It had been incredibly demanding time, but it was worth it. She had definitely chosen Penzance for a purpose and I was more certain than ever that all that had taken place had in some way been preordained.

I was deep in thought and must have been standing in the kitchen for twenty minutes or so when David came in.

'I think Louise needs to come into the hospice for a few days, Philip. She probably needs a blood transfusion, she's very anaemic. We need to get some red blood cells into her, she's terribly weak.'

I told David that I thought that she wouldn't want to do that. She had been through enough already and perhaps it might be better to leave things be.

'You're right, Philip, she doesn't want to come in, but she's really looking forward to seeing Diana again. She'll be here in just over two weeks time. Louise might not make it without some sort of physical boost, a transfusion will give her some energy.'

I told David we would think about it and that we were all too tired to make any decisions, particularly important ones like that.

'You've got to get a break, Philip, you're both driving your-selves too hard. If Louise was away for just a few nights…'

I stopped him in his tracks.

'It's her decision, David, I'll speak to her.'

David left and I went back into the living room. Louise was lying in the green chair looking tired and forlorn.

'Daddy, I'm not going into that fucking charnel house, I'm not ready to die yet.'

I explained to her that her red blood cells needed replenishing and she began to cry softly.

'What's the point if I'm going to die soon anyway, I can't walk any more and I'm tired of this pain. I've had enough.'

I told her that Diana would be coming back soon and that we were going to have a tremendous day. Louise smiled through her tears.

'How long would I have to stay in there, Daddy?'

'Not long, Louise, not long,' I lied.

She looked away from me.

'Will I still be able to do my radio show tomorrow?' she asked.

I looked at her, she was in a pitiful state. She was horribly underweight, deathly pale and by now almost completely paralysed from the waist down. Worse still her sight was now deteriorating by the day. Just as Dr Rao had predicted the cancer had twisted itself around her spine and crept its way to her brain. And yet from time to time her strength returned, her eyes lit up and her spirit still sometimes soared.

*

Radio Wave was the local station in Blackpool. They had adopted Louise's cause with fervour a year before and we had got to know their team quite well. One presenter in particular, Jon Culshaw, had taken to Louise and some time during the early summer he had proposed that Louise present a show of her favourite music. For one reason or another we had not got around to doing this, but Louise was set on the idea. Given her terrible physical state I very much doubted that she could make her date with Jon the following day. Presenting radio shows is, believe it or not, quite an energetic business. I had been in that studio doing fund-raising shows and had always felt drained afterwards. I had watched the young presenters cueing records and advertisements, interviewing guests, running competitions and making small talk. I very much doubted that a young woman in the late stages of terminal cancer would even make it to the studio, let alone present a live one hour shown on a Saturday night at peak listening time.

On the day following our return from Cornwall Louise awoke quite refreshed after a reasonable night's sleep. She dozed for much of the day, and at about 6 p.m. she began to try to prepare herself for her planned 9 p.m. to 10 p.m. slot on local radio. A number of friends visited us that evening and simply could not believe that Louise was actually going to go ahead with this. Uncle Chris in particular was pacing the floor nervously trying to tell himself that everything was going to be all right.

By the time Louise was ready to leave with Judy there was quite a gathering of friends, and a party atmosphere began to develop. Louise was enjoying all the attention as everybody joked about what a mess she was going to make of it all. I wheeled her to the car at 8 p.m. and as I lifted her from her chair I smiled at her.

'You don't have to do this, Louise. Jon has alternative plans if you don't make it. You won't be letting anyone down.'

She tried to look at me through her unseeing eyes.

'Make sure you're listening, Daddy,' she said, 'just make sure you're listening, and tell Chris he's behaving like an old woman!'

Judy drove her the two miles to the radio station and I switched on the radio and tuned in to 96.5 FM to listen to what I was convinced would be a debacle.

The scene in our living room was akin to that which must have been reproduced around the country between 1939 and 1945 as families gathered anxiously around radio sets for news of the war. Uncle Chris, in particular, was on tenterhooks. He was pacing about the room drinking a can of beer.

'She's not well enough to be doing this. Bloody media types, why can't they leave her alone?'

The minutes ticked quickly by and at 8.59 p.m. the departing DJ announced that in one minute a sensational new presenter, Louise Woolcock would be making her debut. My intense apprehension was, by now becoming almost panic – what if she vomits on air or, worse still, collapses or swears!

At 9 p.m. precisely Louise's jingle came on. I held my breath; everything went silent and then to my relief one of Louise's favourite David Bowie songs began to play. As soon as it finished another song began. It was 9.05 p.m. and still no sign of Louise. And suddenly at the end of the second record she burst upon the airwaves, that unmistakable voice, but full of power, laughter and enthusiasm.

'Good evening, everybody, this is Louise Woolcock here...'

For the next hour we sat in thrall. She was magnificent. She laughed, she joked, she played her favourite music. She was a complete professional. I watched Chris shaking his head in disbelief.

'She's a bloody star, where on earth does she get it from?'

I felt so proud as I listened on that warm summer night for I knew just how deep she had had to dig and I think I knew why. Something very special had once again emerged from that cancer-wracked body, she was not giving up yet.

By the time the car pulled into the drive we were feeling quite elated, and as Louise emerged through the front door we were in celebratory mood. As I poured Judy a glass of wine in the kitchen she related the behind the scenes story of this amazing radio show. Louise had begun to vomit as soon as the show went on air and thereafter during some of the records. She had, nonetheless, refused to let any of this affect her, and each time she went on air she seemed to draw from deep within her an amazing strength. In two weeks time she would have to find that strength all over again for the performance of her life.

Chapter Eight

Two or three days after that show Louise was admitted to Trinity Hospice for the first time. She badly needed a blood transfusion to attempt to counter her emaciated state. For our part we badly needed some respite from the twenty-four hour care that Louise had needed for the last two months. She was assigned room three at Trinity. It overlooked a small rose garden in a quiet part of the building. When I visited her shortly after her admission she was a little fretful and apprehensive about her forthcoming transfusion.

The transfusion was delayed that afternoon due to the difficulty of finding enough blood to match Louise's quite rare B positive group. I sat with her as she drifted in and out of consciousness and felt content that she was in good hands. I held her hand as the morphine did its work, and even when she slept I kept talking to her. She often floated back from deep sleep into semi-consciousness and as she did she would try to look at me through her drugs and partial blindness. As she tried to focus she sort of smiled. 'Oh, Daddy, what larks, what larks.' And then as I squeezed her hand in attempted reassurance, 'Ouch, you fucking fool!'

Once again I became a five-year-old incompetent apologising as Louise smiled sleepily and shook her head.

The next few days were very different from the previous two months. For the first time in a long time we were not woken up by Louise's pitiful cries in the early hours, but we had become used to being woken in such fashion and so we didn't sleep very well. I used to wake with a jolt at two or three in the morning and then feel guilty because she wasn't there. I felt that we were avoiding our responsibilities and I wanted her back at home. I convinced myself that I didn't mind spending night after night tossing and turning as she cried out for me and even when I managed sleep I dreamed that she was crying out and so rest had become impossible. I had become used to sitting in the kitchen at three a.m. drinking a lonely vodka or taking twenty mgs of temazepam to try to induce sleep or at least unconsciousness.

Whenever I visited her I felt this terrible guilt; and then one afternoon I went to see her and she was crying bitterly. On her right shoulder was a huge piece of gauze dressing taped into place with elastoplast. The gauze was soaked in blood. She looked at me uncomprehendingly, the nurse in her room looked equally pained. I asked her what had happened. She was drowsy but she managed to tell me that she had had her blood transfusion. It looked to me like a cock up and I went home to telephone Dr Rao at Christie. He seemed very concerned. 'I'm on my way,' he said.

This was strange, indeed. Dr Rao was the oncologist on Christie children's ward, his time was precious but there was no doubt or hesitation in his voice. He was on his way to see Louise to sort things out and I thanked God for this intervention for Louise had expressed to me that she had felt abandoned by the staff at Christie. There was, of course, no reason or logic to this. She had bonded strongly with Dr Rao and his team and she was feeling that she had now been passed on to die in the care of others.

By the time I had returned to Trinity not only had Dr Rao arrived but he was accompanied by Sister Pauline and Wendy, and Louise was content once more. These were the people who really mattered to her. She had placed her trust in these people and they had never let her down, and here they were again making a fuss of her and I loved them for it. The bloody mess which was Louise's shoulder was not the result of a cock up. Nothing much worked in her body any more and attempts at transfusion had simply been messy. Nonetheless, I could not help but reflect just how much her shoulder looked like all those wounded shoulders I had seen in 'B' movie westerns when I was a child.

Diana was due at Trinity in four days time. We proposed that, given her very weak condition, Louise should stay in the hospice until after the royal visit. Louise was not pleased with this suggestion and argued that she would be better off at home. We finally persuaded her to stay, explaining that she needed round the clock care and that we would be there for her in shifts for most of the time. I think that the clincher was the fact that she really did want to be as strong as possible on the 28 July. She desperately wanted to see Diana again.

★

I was sitting with Louise in her hospice room the following afternoon; she was sleeping fitfully and I was enjoying a large vodka and tonic purloined from the patients' drinks trolley, when I noticed a distinct change of atmosphere in the hospice. The atmosphere was becoming more urgent, more charged. People began to bustle rather than stroll and orders began to be given as floors began to gleam and rose bushes were pruned assiduously. Nurses' uniforms looked somehow smarter and David Cooper spent a lot of his time pointing at things. Then later that day a very drowsy Louise pulled at my sleeve.

'Daddy, why are they painting those stones white?' she giggled weakly.

I thought that she was hallucinating again. But no, sure enough I looked to where Louise was pointing and I saw the figure of a man kneeling in the rose garden and he was indeed applying two coats of white emulsion to a row of stones!

'The Princess is really coming, Louise, they wouldn't do this for anyone else – it'll be the bloody roses next.'

And so for the next three days things were cordoned off with red and white tape, more white stones appeared and David Cooper continued to point even more urgently at everything and nothing; and in the middle of all this frenzied activity Louise grew dramatically weaker as each day passed. We seriously began to wonder whether she would emerge alive from each long morphine sleep. Her breathing became noisy and very laboured, and periods of consciousness became shorter and fewer.

As I watched her hovering between life and death I thought many things but I don't think I ever contemplated a life without her. Often I sat in her room with Judy or Uncle Chris and sometimes I looked at their faces, as they must have been looking at mine. They looked bewildered and unable to comprehend this awful reality, just like me. A kind of disbelief had descended upon us all. Louise was too important, too beautiful, she must be immortal, she can't just die, that would be too ordinary, too final. And so we gawped at that which was too frightening to contemplate seriously, and our unspeaking faces said it all.

I met David Cooper at about eight-thirty on the morning of the 28 July. I had been to see Louise, but she was in a deep sleep. We spent some time at reception with some police officers who were organising the Princess's security that day. I remember red and white cordons and crackling radios, but my thoughts were with a desperately ill young woman in room three who had brought all this about. She was lying in her room fighting for her life as dignitaries in suits and uniforms patrolled and discussed and pointed in an important kind of way. As I watched them I smiled inwardly as I thought of how Louise might have viewed this whole situation. When David gave me my badge telling me who I was I smiled at him too, but it was a different kind of smile – I actually felt sorry for him. I realised, of course, that this entire charade was necessary and expected. What I could not have realised on that morning was that Diana shared my cynicism.

I think that Diana was due to arrive at Trinity at about 1 p.m. or perhaps 1.30 p.m. My overriding memory, though, is of Louise. She had spent a terrible night, and at around midday I remember standing by the bed whilst Sister Helen and Judy tried to manoeuvre her into her wheelchair. It was impossible; she was in far too much pain. She cried out mercilessly whenever they tried to lift her from her bed. We gave her yet more morphine and she drifted into a deep sleep. We left her for a while in the vain hope that when she awoke she might have some energy, or at least less pain.

She woke an hour later and she was worse. Now she was vomiting as well. David came into the room. We were fortunate; the Princess was going to be late. Louise looked ghastly. David looked at her.

'Perhaps it might be better if Diana visits her in her room,' he said.

She sat up on one elbow and glared at David.

'I'm getting up to meet Diana, this is my day, I'll be out in a few minutes.'

At that moment I knew she would make it, for I had heard that tone before.

After a monumental struggle, from which I was necessarily excluded for reasons of decency, Louise emerged dreadfully white and trembling. She smiled in my direction as Helen pushed her along the corridor in a heavily padded wheelchair.

'I'm off to meet my public, Daddy, I'm not lurking in my room.' Judy followed closely, looking shattered. It had been one hell of a struggle to get her dressed. They had finally managed to dull her pain with morphine, but I doubted she could stay conscious for the next hour. I imagined all the farcical permutations as Diana performed the opening ceremony. Would Louise fall out of her chair? Would she fall asleep? Would she fall into a coma? It was all possible. I looked at the ceiling in the corridor. 'Please God, just one hour, just one more hour.'

We wheeled her to the hospice reception area. We were possibly the last to arrive. There was a straight line of officials and dignitaries standing at the main entrance where Diana was expected to arrive. We took our place near the end of the line. It began in order of importance, with the High Sheriff of Lancashire followed by the Chairman of Hospice, Dr Cooper, Matron, Bursar etc., and then us. I think we were, in fact, next to the last, Dr Cooper's wife being at the very end, strangely apart from her husband.

Helen and Judy cast nervous glances at one another as Louise rocked forward in her chair momentarily. I glanced out of the window. It was a bright, clear and very hot July day and the crowd awaiting the arrival of the Princess of Wales was enormous. There was a low murmur of anticipation outside as the crowd craned their necks trying to get a faint glimpse of the expected motorcade. I cast my mind back to that first visit. Things had turned around completely from twelve months ago. I thought about the look she had given me as she left that day, 'Write to me, Philip.'

Well, I'd done that and this was the encore, but in a very different performance.

The low murmur outside turned into a buzz and then I heard a ripple of applause, which quickly became a wave. The crowd began to cheer and the line of dignitaries began to adjust their ties and badges. I distinctly remember the High Sheriff fiddling with his sword and looking very hot and uncomfortable in his heavy, much decorated ceremonial uniform. The temperature was in the high eighties and I thought about an anecdote that his delightful wife had related to me not an hour before. Yes, I thought, I was glad for his sake that he was wearing pop socks beneath his heavy cavalry boots!

Before we knew it Diana was shaking hands with the High Sheriff and making small talk. She looked radiant and very alert. As she moved along the line I noticed that each individual lit up visibly and became animated in her company. There was a kind of electricity about her and she emanated great energy and warmth. I quickly recalled my own experience upon meeting her twelve months before, and I knew exactly what each person was feeling as they were introduced – they each felt like the most important person in the world for that brief moment, and they loved it. As she moved nearer to us her eyes began to flash towards Louise. She looked concerned and a little shocked. She seemed to be steeling herself for their second meeting, preparing to meet a young woman who was so obviously close to death whilst she herself was so obviously full of life. Their positions this time could not have been more different.

'Hello again, old friend,' she said and smiled radiantly, but there was a modicum of pity in her face. 'Good gracious, I couldn't miss you with those bright clothes on!'

In spite of her illness Louise had insisted upon wearing her brightest oranges, yellows and reds.

'You made it, then, Louise, you built your hospice. You finally did it, I'm so proud of you.'

She turned towards me and took my hand.

'And you too, Philip, well done, I think you're all marvellous, you've achieved so much.'

I thanked her for coming and made small talk about how well she looked, but all the while she kept glancing at Louise who was staring straight ahead, smiling. At that moment, to her horror, I think Diana realised that Louise was nearly blind. She bent down and whispered something in Louise's ear; they both giggled.

'I'll see you later, Louise,' she said, and with that the Princess was whisked away in a sea of suits for a tour of the hospice.

This was all part of the itinerary. She would take a guided tour of the main building and then enter the new day hospice via a link corridor for the opening ceremony. I watched her in the distance and noticed that her guides, of whom there seemed to be quite a few, were all pointing in different directions at the same time.

We now had a choice. It was ordained that we would meet Diana on a specially erected stage beneath the plaque she was to unveil in the day hospice. We could wheel Louise through the main building whilst Diana was visiting the wards, or we could take her outside and around the main building and into the new day hospice. I asked her which way she wanted to go.

'I want to go outside, Daddy, it's a lovely warm day and I haven't been out for so long; let's go around the outside way, I've spent enough time in here.'

And so Helen turned the chair around and we pushed Louise towards the main exit and outside into the bright sunshine for a three minute walk to the opening ceremony.

As we emerged from the main door there was a huge roar from the crowd. For a minute I thought that Diana had, for some reason, followed us outside, and I looked over my shoulder to check. It was then that I heard loud voices from within the roaring and applauding crowd.

'Well done, Louise.'

'You did it, well done.'

'You're a star.'

The applause became louder as we walked along the length of the crowd. Individuals shouted for photos and for Louise to come closer.

'Take me to my public, Helen,' she said half mockingly.

And Helen did just that. It was the most moving moment of my life as I watched Louise reach out her wasted pale hand. It seemed that everyone wanted to touch her. The crowd was ecstatic. The shouts and applause continued to ring out as we made our way slowly to the Louise Woolcock Day Hospice. I began to notice individual faces in the crowd and many of them were in tears as they cheered her on. By the time we re entered the building Helen, Judy and I were in the same state. We too had been swept along by the wonderful tide of emotion. The people of the Fylde had not come that day to see one princess but two.

We manhandled Louise and her wheelchair onto the small stage and there she sat beneath the small red velvet curtains that covered the plaque. But we were far from alone, there must have been over a hundred important people standing in this large room. The men wore grey suits and the women big hats. Through the centre of this long room was cordoned off a narrow pathway along which Diana would emerge to sit beside Louise on the stage. There was an expectant but subdued buzz from this indoor crowd. The whole thing reminded me of an end of term school assembly. I pulled up a chair and sat beside Louise, holding her hand. Every now and again a specially invited suit or hat glanced towards us. These were glances of pity, admiration and curiosity and every so often a camera flashed from the press area to the side of us.

Louise began to become drowsy after about five minutes.

'Come on, Louise,' I whispered urgently, 'come on, don't go to sleep, not in front of this lot, let them see you winning. Think of something funny. Come on, smile, look at those hats, that's enough to make anyone laugh.'

She began to giggle and squeezed my hand. I began to describe some of the hats.

'Stop it, Daddy, we're supposed to be serious today, just shut up about fucking hats.'

The mood of the crowd changed audibly; there was a short period of silence and almost at once heads turned to face up the pathway. Diana was on her way and hats and suits alike began to applaud politely as she made her way towards Louise. As she did so I moved quickly off the stage to join Judy and Helen a few feet away. There were only going to be two princesses sitting on that tiny stage that day. Diana sat down beside Louise, placed her hand on hers and leaned over to whisper confidentially in her ear. Louise smiled as Diana squeezed her hand reassuringly.

The Chairman of Hospice Governors mounted the stage and took his place in front of the microphone.

'Ladies and gentlemen, we are proud today…'

I prayed for him to be brief, but chairmen of things so rarely are. Diana knew this and began to glance at Louise nervously. Ten minutes went by and he was still in full flow. Louise's eyes began to close, she rocked forward gently. Diana squeezed her hand once again and began to look concerned. She leaned over and whispered to Louise again. Her eyes opened and she smiled. Thank God, I thought, but this man was not for stopping. He ploughed on relentlessly for what seemed an age until finally I sensed with great relief that he was winding down. It was Diana's turn now and as the applause died away she stood up and moved quickly towards the veiled plaque. As she did so David Cooper stepped from beside me to place a beautiful engraved cut glass rose bowl in Louise's lap. Diana was mercifully quick. Just a few well chosen words and a well practised pull of the cords. The tiny curtains opened. The silver plaque gleamed. The hats and suits applauded and in a flash she was back sitting next to Louise. As the applause died down Louise tried in vain to lift the beautiful rose bowl from her lap to present to the Princess, but she simply couldn't raise it more than a few inches (it weighed about two pounds). David Cooper moved the few feet onto the stage and helped her pass it over to Diana. The Princess placed it in her lap and gave Louise another concerned look, she then looked at the piece of glassware and threw up her hands in pleasant surprise.

'Louise, it's got your name on it, I'll treasure it for ever; but I'll never get all my cornflakes in it!'

She whispered something else to Louise and they both began to laugh. Diana glanced across the room to a spot just over my shoulder. Some sort of signal was given and she got to her feet. Diana bent down and whispered in Louise's ear yet again. Louise smiled contentedly; she placed her hand on Louise's and I watched her hand tense as she squeezed; Louise winced a little and Diana mouthed some words to her.

'Okay, I'll come with you, then,' Louise said.

Diana looked upset.

'I wish you could, Louise, I so wish that you could.'

She turned away to leave and I noticed that her eyes were filling up. The Princess of Wales was about to cry in public and my heart went out to her.

We wheeled Louise out to see Diana off. She slid into the back of the green Jaguar and as the car pulled away she looked sad and thoughtful. She turned as the car went past and gave Louise a long look, then she was gone.

We took Louise back to her room. She seemed happy and a little pensive.

'I'm so tired, Daddy,' she said, 'wasn't that wonderful.'

Judy and Helen lifted her onto her bed and I left the room. People were drifting around the building and some remained in the day hospice drinking warm white wine. It was late afternoon but the sun was still hot. I heard the purr of Mick's Bentley as it approached the hospice entrance, and I went to get Judy. Helen was giving Louise some medication. 'Don't be long, Mummy,' she said.

Judy looked as tired as Louise but she promised to return to the hospice later.

We went home and reflected on another exceptional day. Diana had shown Louise a lot of attention, but more than that she had shown obvious concern. She could not have failed to be moved by what she saw and I was certain that the impression of a strong young woman facing death so bravely and without complaint had struck a chord somewhere deep within Diana's psyche. Judy returned to the hospice at about 7 p.m. as promised and I set about preparing Louise's room for her return the next morning. She had been pleading to come home for two or three days, and in spite of the obvious difficulties we agreed that she could, and we were glad.

★

It was probably about 8.30 p.m. or even 9 p.m. I remember it was beginning to get dark and I was sitting alone in the kitchen smoking a cigarette, the boys were watching TV. There was an atmosphere of gloom in the house because we all felt that now Louise had seen Diana again she would probably give up the uneven struggle and quietly die. I didn't hear the phone at first and when I did I felt reluctant to answer it. I was tired of explaining to people just how ill Louise was, I lifted the receiver wearily, perhaps Judy had decided to spend the night with Louise.

'Could I speak to Philip Woolcock, please.'

The voice was clear and familiar,

'Speaking,' I said suddenly much more alert as I realised with a start just who this might be.

'It's Diana here, Philip. I hope I'm not disturbing you.'

My reply was stuttered and probably incoherent as my body found adrenaline it didn't know it had.

'How are you all coping, I was so pleased to be able to see Louise today. She's terribly ill isn't she?'

I explained that Louise would live for only a few more days and that she was coming home tomorrow. I spoke of how tired we were and how happy Louise had been to see her. I could tell that Diana was very moved. She spoke of Louise's tremendous courage and asked me how much pain she was in. I talked about the difficulty of pain control, of paralysis and Diana interjected, 'She's also blind, isn't she?'

She sounded very upset, and I detected a quiver of emotion in her voice as she asked more searching questions. Before I knew it I was saying goodbye. As I put the phone down I felt strangely elated, but hardly surprised by this tremendous gesture of compassion. I had sensed earlier that day that Diana had wanted to talk. Unfortunately, schedules and itinerary forbade proper conversation. She had been on the telephone for perhaps ten minutes, but it felt longer. That call was to keep me going during the frightening days that lay ahead.

Judy returned about an hour later. Like me she seemed to have run out of adrenaline. She looked dreadful and I wondered how much more she could take. She had been preparing for her heart to be broken for too long; she had been watching her precious first born child wither and fade, and, like me, she could not accept that the inevitable was, in fact, inevitable. Judy was both lifted and heartened upon hearing of Diana's call. The fact that somebody so much in the public eye had taken precious time to speak to a family in such pain seemed to confirm to her that perhaps the world was not so bad after all and that there was another side to pain and suffering. I poured her a large drink and we began to plan for Louise's return home for however long.

The next day we went to see Louise. She was dozing in a large chair that was facing the rose garden. She was somewhere between waking and sleep as was so often the case following morphine. She smiled as I pulled up a chair beside her and told her of Diana's call the night before.

'I knew she would, Daddy, I just knew she would,' she said and began to chuckle to herself.

I realised that Diana must have told her she was going to call during one of those whispered confidences the day before. No wonder they were giggling, they were planning a surprise and probably anticipating my reaction. This was very like Louise, she loved to surprise and shock.

'Daddy, I'm definitely going home today, aren't I? You promised I could.'

I looked at her closely: her gums were bleeding and causing her teeth to be stained, her pale yellow skin was stretched tight across her cheekbones and she was not looking at me but at a spot somewhere between the two of us, trying desperately to make out my outline.

I took her hand.

'Of course you're coming home, Louise, we promised. How do you feel?'

'Just tired, Daddy after yesterday. It was wonderful, wasn't it? I just wish I wasn't so sleepy all the time.' She turned her head to face me once again. 'Take me to see my plaque, Daddy. I'd love to see my plaque.'

I called for Helen and between us we lifted her into her wheelchair. I pushed her out of her room and along the corridor towards what was now 'The Louise Woolcock Day Hospice'.

The day hospice was deserted and I manoeuvred Louise towards her silver plaque, she looked intently in the direction of the plaque and I lifted her pale skeletal hand and placed her fingers on the engraved words. I watched as she moved her beautifully tapered fingers along each letter of her name. She smiled with satisfaction.

'We did it, Daddy, Diana was right: we should be very proud.' She kept her hand resting against the plaque seemingly in deep contemplation before declaring her intention to return home. 'Right, Daddy, let's go home, get me an ambulance, I'm going back to my room now to get ready.'

I spoke to David Cooper and he organised an ambulance to bring her home later that afternoon.

'You're going to need a lot of help, Philip. Louise needs round the clock nursing now, I'll arrange for a Macmillan nurse to come tonight and sit with her so you'll be able to get some rest.'

I told David that we would be fine, but when I popped my head around Louise's door to say goodbye I shuddered inside at the prospect of her returning to us, and wondered whether even the three mile ambulance journey home might be too much for her.

I was sitting in the kitchen sipping an over-large vodka and tonic when I heard the ambulance pull up outside. By the time I got to the front door the two ambulance men were cheerily lifting Louise on a stretcher out of the back and as they moved her expertly out I noticed that even the slightest bump made her grimace with pain. She looked at me apprehensively as if fearing that they would drop her completely. She tried to smile as they lowered the stretcher to carrying height.

'I'm home at last, Daddy,' she said, and I noticed that her voice was quite faint in the outside air, more like a hoarse whisper completely devoid of any strength.

My mind drifted back to the days when she had bounded energetically from her school taxi and positively shrieked her arrival through the house, looking deeply tanned with her blonde streaked curls, bouncing enthusiastically down the hallway; her face lit, eyes on fire as she began to relate some tale of misdemeanour committed during period five. Now she lifted her hand and squeezed my finger as she was carried inside by her 'escorts.' As she tried to smile deep creases appeared at the side of her mouth as her tight pallid skin stretched across her teeth. I resolved as I tucked her into bed that afternoon that I would never let her have access to a mirror.

She was soon asleep and I returned to my bottle of vodka. I knew deep in my heart that drinking large vodka and tonics at 4 p.m. was not going to solve anything. But the alcohol did take away that terrible and sometimes unbearable persistent pain, albeit temporarily, and even that small relief was better than nothing at all. It also had the added advantage of allowing me to snatch short sleeps throughout the day, thus removing me temporarily from my purgatory.

As evening approached Louise awoke and asked to come down into the living room. We piled the settee high with bolsters and pillows and I carried her downstairs. By the time I had made her comfortable she was breathing very heavily and trembling slightly. Within twenty minutes she was twisting in agony as the pain took hold again. We gave her morphine and she promptly threw up. We waited and gave her more until she was drowsy again. Soon she fell into a deep, hideous sleep. Open mouthed, lungs rattling, sometimes crying out in pain or drug-induced nightmare. I sat and watched, and as I held her hand I was very tempted to place a pillow over her face and end this torture for us all. I was certain by now that this would not have been wrong, but I doubted that I could have persisted if she had struggled. Instead, I poured another large drink. One or two friends dropped by to see her, and I poured yet more drink.

At about ten o'clock the doorbell rang. As I stared at the rather formidable looking Macmillan nurse I tried to speak some words of welcome (even though I had forgotten that she was coming).

'Hello,' she said, 'I'm Audrey Tebay. I'll be looking after Louise tonight.'

I invited her into the kitchen 'Thish ish where we keep the tea,' I slurred. I tried to explain some other simple routines before giving in to reality. 'I'm sho shorry, nursh but I'm completely pished!'

She looked at me sternly and, I sensed for a moment, disapprovingly. Then she smiled a lovely warm smile as she placed a reassuring hand on mine.

'I don't blame you, love,' she said, 'I don't blame you at all. So would I be in your situation. Now sit down and I'll make us a nice cup of tea.'

Judy walked into the kitchen at that moment and I felt relieved. At least she'll see that one of us is fit to be in charge of the house, I thought. I clumsily introduced Audrey to my wife.

'Thish ish Audrey,' I mumbled incoherently, whilst trying to light a cigarette.

'I'm sho pleashed you're here,' said Judy grasping the radiator for support as she swayed to and fro.

I glanced at the litre bottle of vodka, it was empty!

I awoke the following morning with a start. There was a faint tapping on the bedroom door. I looked at my watch it was exactly 7.30 a.m. I had no idea who could possibly be on the other side of our bedroom door but I instinctively shouted 'come in.' Audrey appeared bearing a tray of tea. I had forgotten all about her as the alcohol had done its work. It was not every morning that a sixty-year-old woman entered my bedroom smiling profusely, bearing cups of tea. I felt profoundly embarrassed and began to apologise for my having been so tired and emotional the night before. She brushed aside my pathetic schoolboy attempts at self-justification by explaining that Louise had had a very restful night, and apart from the need for two doses of morphine, she had slept well. It occurred to me, as the last remnants of Smirnoff cleared from my befuddled brain, that this delightful and thoroughly dedicated woman had spent the whole night sitting beside my daughter to allow us some rest.

I remonstrated that she should have woken us sooner in order that we might have relieved her. She smiled as she sat sipping her tea.

'It was a pleasure, Philip, she's a remarkable young woman is Louise – a remarkable woman. Now I must get going, it's nearly eight o'clock. I'll be back again at ten tonight.'

She left the room and I wanted to go after her and hug her, for she had given me something beyond price. It was the first full night's sleep we had enjoyed for two whole months, and, in spite of a raging headache, I felt much better.

Louise woke an hour or so later.

'Has Audrey gone yet, Daddy?' she said. 'Isn't she lovely? We spent some time talking when I couldn't sleep. I was telling her about everything, especially Diana and the fund-raising.'

I looked around the room, Audrey's chair was still by Louise's bed, together with awaiting sick bowls and tissues. On Louise's dressing table there was a cheque for fifty pounds made out to 'The Louise Woolcock Cancer Support Fund' signed Audrey Tebay. Audrey had donated her hard-earned wages to Louise's fund.

Later that day Fred came round. He too looked tired; he had spend many hours with us, sometimes just sitting, sometimes talking, but always around when we most needed him. Today, however, he had a specific purpose. For some weeks Louise had been speaking about the nature and meaning of God. She had been trying to come to terms with some very profound questions. She had spoken to Fred about faith and had, after long consideration, expressed a desire to be anointed in the Catholic faith. As a Catholic by birth I had felt pleased by this decision, but had been determined to allow Louise to find her own way, and so had played little or no part in her private discussions with Fred.

I carried her into the living room and made her as comfortable as possible whilst Fred prepared for the ceremony. There were just the three of us in the room, and as Fred performed this very moving ritual I stood beside Louise. She looked very peaceful and the ravages of cancer seemed to lift from her tired features as Fred placed the sign of the cross in wax upon her forehead and palms. It was a very moving ceremony and throughout its duration Louise stared out of the living room window with an expression of great joy and serenity on her face. Her eyes lit up again and she seemed full of emotion. I watched her intently, and to this day I am convinced that she was possessed by something very beautiful and profound. When the ceremony was over Fred knelt beside her.

'I will pray for you, Louise,' he said and placed his hand on hers.

She inclined her head towards him.

'No, Fred, I will pray for you, you are my brother.'

She looked beautifully serene at that moment and her voice was full of certainty and strength. All fear and pain seemed to have been extinguished from her and she seemed at perfect peace. I sat in silence and, to some extent, in awe as Louise was once again claimed by sleep. No morphine this time, though, it was a natural sleep full of contentment and easy breathing. I looked at Fred as he remained kneeling beside her, and he returned my look with a knowing smile. It seemed that none of the magic of that twenty minutes had surprised him. Whatever had made its benign presence felt during that ritual had, I felt, been expected by Fred;

for him this was nothing unusual.

Louise awoke very refreshed in the early evening. She sat up and I noticed the waxen cross on her forehead reflecting the early evening sun. She smiled contentedly and she looked like a saint.

'That was a beautiful sleep, Daddy,' she said. 'Has Fred left yet?'

I told her that Fred had left some hours before.

'I'll miss him,' she said, 'I wish all priests were like that.'

Her features began to crease with pain and she asked for morphine. I poured the colourless, tasteless liquid onto a spoon and held it to her lips while she sipped like a small bird.

'Is Uncle Chris coming tonight, Daddy? It is Saturday, isn't it?'

She sounded unsure.

'Of course, Chris will be here soon.'

She asked me to carry her downstairs in preparation for Chris's arrival. There was something determined in Louise's manner that night; it was as if she had things to do. She spoke a lot about her beloved Chris and was beginning to fret a little when the doorbell rang and Chris pushed through the door as the sound of the bell reverberated through the house. He had been taking Dutch courage in the pub around the corner. He had seen Louise in Trinity only two days before and was apprehensive about how she would fare at home. He had been hurting badly during the last few days.

I had spoken to his mother and she had told me that he had been eating very little and spending a lot of time in the pub. He too looked very tired that evening. A few friends spent the evening with us, but Louise was soon forced to return to her room as the drugs took over. Chris went with her and closed her door behind him. At ten o'clock Audrey Tebay arrived as usual and made herself a cup of tea. I went into the kitchen with her.

'Audrey,' I said tentatively, 'you know when you bring us that tray of tea at 7.30 each morning?' She looked puzzled.

'Go on,' she said. 'Well, can you keep on bringing it at exactly 7.30?' I said. 'I mean, if Louise dies in the night I'll still want you to bring the tea tray in at 7.30.'

'What do you mean?' she said, glancing at the vodka bottle by the kettle.

I clumsily tried to explain to her that I had spent the previous night in a waking nightmare imagining knocks on the bedroom in the small hours and Audrey walking in to announce Louise's death. This had become so bad that I had been waking every half hour in a cold sweat imagining faint knocking on the bedroom door.

Audrey gave me one of her 'eeee love' sort of smiles as she realised what I wanted.

'Whatever happens in the night, Philip, is nothing to do with you. I promise that I will only ever wake you at 7.30.' I thanked her profusely and watched her watching me intently as I poured a large vodka. 'Be careful with that stuff Philip, please be careful.'

'I know what I'm doing, Audrey, don't worry about me.'

She smiled, but some of the warmth in that smile seemed to have been replaced by pity and concern.

While Audrey sipped her tea in the kitchen I slipped upstairs to Louise's room. I quietly opened the door expecting her to be fast asleep. The room was lit by the moon and I made out the figure of Chris sitting on the side of the bed. I had forgotten he had gone up to see her more than an hour before. Louise was sitting propped up by cushions. Chris was holding her hand; they had obviously been enjoying a long conversation. I apologised for interrupting and left, saying that Audrey would be up in ten minutes.

When Chris came into the kitchen, he was deep in thought.

'She's dozed off, Phil,' he said, 'we've just been talking about things.'

I knew exactly what had taken place. Louise had cast her spell and allowed Chris to say goodbye in his own way. I could tell by the look on his face that he knew something significant had taken place and, like me in Cornwall he was trying to take it all in.

'Louise told me we would still have our Byron night,' he said quietly. They had been planning a night of indulgence in the name of their favourite poet for some weeks and Louise's final promise was still echoing in his ears.

'I'm sure you will, Chris,' I said, 'someday.'

I lit him a cigarette and passed him a glass. It was the last time he was ever to see her, and they both knew it.

Chris spent the rest of that night in deep contemplation. We sat in silence in the kitchen drinking until after midnight. I had never seen him looking so tense and utterly distraught. His body was rigid and I could feel the anger and disbelief emanating from him.

'I'm going now, old chap,' he said stiffly. 'Maybe I'll come tomorrow, I'm very tired.' He rose from the kitchen stool and put his hand on my shoulder. 'I'm sorry, Phil, I'm just not up to it. I knew I couldn't hack it.'

This was a ridiculous statement, but typical of Chris. He was and is the most self-deprecating man I have ever met.

I slept very little on that awful Saturday night. I didn't wait for Audrey's 7.30 call. I got up at 5 a.m. It was still dark and I sat in the living room trying to make sense of everything. I could hear Louise moaning and crying out quietly in her sleep and I wanted to end it all. I heard Audrey trying to comfort her, but to little or no avail. She was obviously in terrible pain and was probably hallucinating under the influence of a whole cocktail of drugs.

As the dawn broke I heard a gentle knock on the kitchen door. It was David Cooper. I made some coffee and we both stood in the kitchen in silence. I sensed that he was agitated. He asked me what sort of a night Louise had had and I explained the night terrors, the hallucinating and the terrible cries of anguish that came as she realised, during mercifully brief moments of lucidity, that she was soon going to die. No words of comfort could assuage any of this and I felt useless. I knew we were shortly going to lose her and I hadn't even thought about saying goodbye, a part of me was still refusing to face reality. Instead, I retreated into the past, a much happier and safer place. That way at least I could maintain my sanity.

'How much longer can she go on, David?' I asked, almost absent mindedly.

I wasn't looking at him, I daren't.

'I think you can answer that question yourself, Philip, you only have to look at her. It's only the steroids that are keeping her alive,' he said. 'What do you want me to do?' I looked at David and he returned my look without flinching. 'Philip, she could go on like this for days. She's young, her heart is strong.'

I felt numb and physically sick. It was as if he were talking about an animal, a much-loved pet. I wouldn't allow any pet, no matter how loved to go through this slow tortuous hell. Louise was in emotional and physical agony. She couldn't walk, see, eat or sleep, and worst of all she was often fully aware of everything that was happening to her. How many times had she said to me that she was afraid of death, afraid also that her young brothers might find her dead? That was one of her greatest fears. Even at the point of death she was thinking of others.

'It wouldn't be right, Daddy, they shouldn't have to go through that on top of everything else.'

How many times during the last few days as she had lain sleeping had I sat wishing that each laboured breath would be her last? The tumours by now were everywhere, a new one had appeared just beneath her collar bone only the night before.

There was a moments silence before David spoke.

'It's only the steroids that are keeping her alive and they are causing side effects. We have to withdraw the steroids, nature will take over.' I watched my tears drop onto the kitchen floor and felt myself beginning to shake. 'It's not just about Louise, Philip, look at what this is doing to you all.'

Of course, David was right. For almost three years now we had lived with terminal cancer. It's shadow had cast itself over us even during times of intense joy and happiness. For long periods it had retreated until it was almost out of sight, but we always knew it was there and would be back to destroy us. It was always just a matter of time. For the last three months we had lived in hell, unable to do anything, as we watched Louise desperately fighting a losing battle. The moments of tremendous courage and selflessness that she had shown had only served to make things more painful, for they reminded us of her exceptional beauty, of the magnitude of what we were about to lose. I told David that as ever Louise would make any decisions about whether or not she would return to Trinity. Knowing Louise I somehow knew that she would know when the time would be right. Many things that had happened had begun to convince me that so much of all this was strangely preordained. I agreed with David that to withdraw her steroids would constitute an act of kindness. But how and when? I didn't want to think about that.

David left soon afterwards. Audrey had also gone. She must have seen us in close conversation and just slipped off. I sat in the kitchen for a while trying to take in everything we had said and was wondering how things would be in the end when I heard Louise calling faintly, 'Daddy, can you bring me a drink?'

I took her a glass of juice containing about a fluid ounce. I had become used to working in these small amounts by now. It was like feeding a very small child. As I entered her room I noticed a sinister new development. Her right eye was horribly bruised as if she had had a nasty fall. I was about to call for Judy when I realised that the pressure of her brain tumour must have caused the blood vessels behind her eye to haemorrhage. I quietly cursed this unrelenting and vile disease, and simultaneously felt pleased that when she died it could do no more: it would die with her. I had reached the point where her terrible suffering had become unbearable to me. The rest of that day was just a blur of sick bowls, tears, people visiting and looking shocked, endless cigarettes and a feeling of utter helplessness. Louise's body seemed now to be disintegrating by the day. For the last fortnight some new tumour or new complication had asserted itself, and each day we somehow found the will and energy to cope, to alleviate pain and distress, to reassure to hug and to show our love in so many ways.

On Monday 3 August Louise awoke feeling strangely refreshed. I remember her sitting up in bed in her primrose pyjamas with her black eye. For some reason we were alone in the house. I went to sit on the bed with her to try to assess her immediate needs. Her lips were bloody, dry and cracked and her voice very weak. I brought her a sip of water and held her hand whilst I placed the glass to her lips.

'How are you feeling today Louise?'

It was by now a rhetorical question which always engendered the same response.

'I'm okay, Daddy, what larks!'

This response in turn was usually followed by a twisting of her features as the first pain of the new day kicked in and then a retching as her cancerous stomach rejected whatever liquid we had managed to get that far (by now a lot of water or juice dribbled down her chin – her coordination had been destroyed by her brain tumour). On this morning she seemed free of pain and successfully drank a small amount of mineral water. She smiled at me as I examined her damaged eye.

'What's wrong, Daddy' she whispered.

'Nothing, Louise, just looking to see if you need your face wiping.'

The eye was much blacker now and the bruise had spread outwards in rings of purple and brown. Louise began to look preoccupied as she often did before launching a bombshell.

'Daddy, I want to go back to my room at the hospice now.'

She was finally ready to die. She had prepared herself; she seemed strangely at peace. I had been told of this by Sister Helen, her nurse. People who were ready to die seem to have prepared themselves, and I knew deep within my heart that she was now ready.

'Call me an ambulance, Daddy, please, I need to leave soon.'

I was on automatic pilot now as I called David at Trinity.

'Her room is waiting, Philip, when she gets here we'll put her on a valium drip to relax her and we'll leave the steroids.'

I hung up and stood for a while in the hallway. I thought of all the times I had picked up that phone to hear her voice from hospital.

'I'm on my way home, Daddy, are you okay?' Or from university: 'Daddy, I'm very drunk, it's fantastic here, are you bringing Uncle Chris on Sunday?'

So many happy calls as her life raced along. So much energy and so many beautiful eccentricities. Her sparkling eyes, her outrageous warm laugh, her tanned skin, lean limbs and cascading streaked curls always tangled and blowing about. What was lying on that bed that day was a shell, all that remained now was debris, the wreckage after the war. Louise was moving on now, and I wasn't ready.

As I pondered all of this I heard the ambulance pull up outside. I knew the ambulance men and I think that they knew exactly what was happening because they didn't seem quite so perky and jokey as they usually were. They took a large stretcher upstairs and I watched as they gingerly lifted her from the bed. Judy was downstairs looking numb. My state of mind was such that I hadn't realised that she was in the house that morning. I began to detach myself from everything that was going on. It was as if I were a spectator. Louise smiled at me as she was carried out of the front door.

'I'll be okay, Daddy, don't worry,' she whispered.

'I'll come and see you just as soon as you're comfortable, Louise,' I replied. 'I just need to sort out what Sam and Barney are going to be doing.'

They opened the rear doors of the ambulance. I think Judy got in first and I stood in the front garden.

As they lifted her into the ambulance I noticed her right hand emerge slowly from beneath the rough red blanket. She raised her thumb and smiled: 'I'll be back, Daddy,' she said, 'I'll be back.'

They were the last words she ever spoke to me. As I watched the ambulance move slowly up the hill and around the corner, I thought of all the times I had stood in exactly the same spot as Judy drove her to Christie. The headscarves, the pale face and the irrepressible smile. The times we had strolled around that corner to meet Uncle Chris in the pub on bright frosty evenings and balmy autumn days. Laughing, always laughing.

I think I was still standing in the front garden when Fred's car pulled up.

'Pheel, I've come to see Louise. What are you doing in the garden?' He looked concerned. 'Are you all right, Pheel,' he said.

I must have been looking thoughtful and shocked at the same time, and I didn't respond to him in the usual ebullient way. We went inside and it occurred to me in a rare moment of inspiration that Fred thought that Louise had died; for by the time we got inside he was looking quite upset and lost for words. He told me later that when he had arrived to find me in the garden I had told him that Louise had gone. I had simply said, 'She's gone, Fred,' and I had looked so forlorn that he had made the obvious assumption. He wasn't heartened by the news that Louise was back in the hospice. Like me, he knew that she had gone there to die, that it was just a matter of time now. The waiting game was about to begin.

Chapter Nine

Judy phoned from the hospice.

'Louise has settled peacefully,' she said.

'Wendy is with me. We'll stay for a while if you'll stay with Sam and Barney. I'll let you know if anything happens.'

I was pleased with this arrangement because at that time I was so bewildered and exhausted I just couldn't face going to see her there and then. I agreed that I would go to the hospice later when Judy returned. The boys were fully aware of what was happening. The pain and tension in the house was palpable and they were dealing with all this in their own way. They had gone out to play.

One of us had to be there, exclusively for them all of the time. I returned to sit with Fred. We sat in silence for a while before he broached the subject I had most dreaded. There was no subtle way of approaching this, no euphemism existed that might help to ease the situation for me. Louise was about to die and she must have a grave. Fred was direct.

'Pheel, you know what comes next, don't you? I presume Louise will need a grave.'

My heart lurched, I felt physically sick upon hearing the words, after all she was still alive as we spoke. But Fred was right; I very much wanted Louise to be buried in the small graveyard at St John's Catholic Church in Poulton. It was a pretty place full of trees.

'I haven't thought about that, Fred,' I lied.

'Come down to the church with me, Pheel, we can sort it out now.'

I think that Fred had been sorting it out for some time; it was his style to sort things out, he was indeed a guardian angel.

I vividly remember driving to St John's Church. We must have been talking for a long time for by now it was getting dark. Judy had phoned me about an hour before saying that Louise was in a deep and peaceful sleep and I had promised to relieve her as soon as I had resolved this grisly business. It was a warm and very windy evening, the sky was dark with foreboding and heavy grey clouds were gliding from the west in the gale. We parked by the church and I was immediately aware of the thunderous roar of the wind in the trees above me. Leaves were being ripped from the branches prematurely as the wind tossed and buffeted the huge oaks and sycamores.

'Come on, Pheel, I'll show you.'

We walked thirty yards down a narrow path to a spot where the gravestones ended abruptly. Fred stopped by the last stone.

'Here, Pheel, just here,' he said and pointed to the damp grass.

So this is where she'll lie for ever, I thought. The place was beneath a huge sycamore tree that roared in the wind above us. As I stood in the dark with Fred my thoughts moved to much happier times. We were crouching together by the River Eamont in Cumbria examining two large brown trout, freshly caught on the fly. Her tiny hands touching their bright speckled flanks. Fingers opening their dead mouths and exploring pink gills. Blond curls cascading into the brambles and nettles. And the sound of that river roaring just like the trees on this awful night. She had learned about death in a very beautiful place. I was learning about it in different circumstances.

I remember we had to go to see a man, a church warden I think, and I had to sign something. He was very kind and I got the feeling we were expected. All the time Fred was there, guiding, comforting and assuring.

'Okay, Pheel, we'll go to Louise now.'

We climbed into his battered blue Polo and drove the two miles through that stormy black night to Trinity. Hospices at night are strange places.

The atmosphere at Trinity was peaceful, the lighting subdued. Every so often as we walked along the carpeted corridor we heard a gentle moan or someone clearing their throat. As we turned into the corridor along which lay Louise's room I became conscious of a noise that still haunts my worst nightmares. From a distance I heard a most horrible and unearthly noise. It was like a malfunctioning and very noisy coffee percolator This sound permeated the whole corridor. As we got close to Louise's room I realised in a moment of horror that this terrible sound was my daughter's death rattle.

As I entered the room a nurse was gently patting her back.

'Can't you stop that fucking noise,' I said as I sensed my anger rising. Fred clutched my arm.

'No Pheel,' he said, 'this is nobody's fault.'

The nurse looked very uncomfortable.

'Leave her,' I said, 'it's okay.'

With each deep breath the noise seemed to become louder like a piercing growl. The nurse explained that this noise was caused by Louise's lungs filling up with fluid. She was in a deep sleep and the nurse had been turning her over to help ease this awful congestion. I became calmer.

'Could you leave us alone now, nurse?' I asked quietly.

Judy had left an hour before to get some rest. It was my turn now. I stood by her bed contemplating her right profile and once again began to drift back to the past. To that cold March day when she had been born. I remember her lying in her incubator struggling for life. On that day I had watched her wriggling and clutching and had greatly admired her left profile. The pretty upturned tiny nose and tiny rosebud lips. No, not much change, I thought, the profile was just the same only this time she was about to die just twenty-one years after that arduous struggle for life. Suddenly the noise was gone. She moaned quietly and I began to talk to her. I told her how much I loved her, that she had become my whole life, that she mustn't fear. I assured her I was with her now. I talked about how the pixies and goblins were with her and that all our larks would be for ever. She stirred slightly and I became conscious of Fred's hand resting on my shoulder.

'Don't stop, Pheel, she's listening to you. See the way her breathing is easier.'

He was right, her breathing had become easier she looked beautiful, full of peace, waxen white, fine boned, more Pre-Raphaelite than ever. She was once again the fairy child of my youth. She had become transformed in the throes of death and I felt small and insignificant. I was going home to continue my mundane existence, she was moving on to something infinitely better.

I spoke to her for a few more minutes about our favourite times and things. Sometimes I laughed and sometimes I sobbed gently as I related our life together and all our larks, and then I felt that I could go on no longer. I found myself telling Louise how I couldn't live without her. I began to ask her not to leave me.

'One day at a time, Louise, come on, one day at a time.'

My tone became pleading.

'Let's just get through today Louise.'

I could feel my tears trickling down my neck. Fred squeezed my shoulder. 'Leave it now, Pheel, you've both had enough.'

I rose up and as I did so Fred knelt in my place and began to offer the last sacraments. He held her thin, pale hand just as he had done during the anointing. The beauty and sheer tragedy of this moment finally reached deep within me. I began to shake as my heart burst. I couldn't let her hear me weeping in this way. I looked at her beautiful pixie face, I stroked her hair, I turned and left that room to collapse in a chair outside.

Kathryn, the deputy Matron was waiting outside. She looked at me in the same way as Jane had done when Dr Rao was giving his fateful prognosis. 'Oh, Philip,' she said 'let go now, just let go.'

And I did, I had to – I sobbed like a tiny child. 'I'm a coward, Kathryn, I'm a fucking coward, I've let her down. I always let her down, I can't go back, I just can't, I've had enough. Don't let her die, please she can't die.'

Kathryn's voice was quiet and controlled.

'You are a very brave man, Philip. You are one of the bravest families I've ever met. Louise is very proud of you. You're deserving of her love, you are not a coward.'

For some reason I hated myself that night. I felt that I ought to be punished for all the pain she had gone through. I felt utterly desolate. The sobbing subsided slightly and Kathryn held both my hands.

'She's not in any pain, Philip, she's very peaceful now.'

Fred appeared at my side.

'Come on, Pheel, let's go home, you must rest. What about Sam and Barney? They're waiting at home for their dad, come on.'

Judy looked wrecked, the boys uncomprehending as I came

into the living room. We just stared at one another.

'What next?' I said to Judy, but she didn't reply.

I could hear the wind roaring pitilessly in the trees behind the house. I went out into the moonless night to sit in the dark and try to collect my thoughts. I had sat on this patio wall many times with Louise in such happy circumstances. I would often sit in this place and hear her taxi pulling away. She would come and sit with me in her pale blue school uniform and talk about her day. She looked so healthy and happy in the hot summer sun; I remember watching her sunbathing on the patio one hot afternoon and thinking that she looked so healthy, vibrant and glowing that she could never die. That was the summer before cancer struck her down and now at the end of her last summer on earth I was sitting alone in the pitch blackness, numb with shock and having run out of days to live one at a time.

I sat there for perhaps half an hour with my thoughts, and every so often I wondered if she had died yet. Somehow I wanted the phone to ring to tell me it was all over, that the husk that was my daughter's body had allowed the spirit to leave. By the time I went inside the boys had gone to bed exhausted. I went upstairs and felt pleased that they were both in a deep sleep, breathing steadily and not stirring. They had had enough of all this, they didn't deserve to have their young lives dominated by the horrors of cancer. Children so young, I thought, have hamsters to teach them about life, death and loss. They were learning in a very cruel way. I went back downstairs and we sat in silence for perhaps twenty minutes. I looked at the clock: it was after 2 a.m. I tried to picture Louise struggling to hold on to life, fighting for every breath, and I felt guilty for being at home. Matron had told me that I was in no fit state to be with Louise, I was too emotionally fragile by now. As the clock ticked and wind relentlessly roared in the trees, we heard the bathroom light switch on. There was always a loud distinctive click as the string was pulled.

'One of the boys is up,' Judy said, 'go and see if they're okay I don't want them to be just lying up there with their thoughts, not tonight.'

I went upstairs, the bathroom light was on and the string switch still swaying silently. I went to the boys room. 'Are you okay boys,' I whispered. 'Do you want to come down for a bit?' I switched on the bedside lamp. Both boys were still as I had left them, in a deep sleep, they had hardly moved. They were both breathing rhythmically almost in unison. There was no doubt about it, neither Sam nor Barney had visited the bathroom, but somebody or something most definitely had. I sensed that Louise had died and I telephoned the hospice. A staff nurse answered.

'Louise is very close to death, Philip,' she said. 'She's in a deep coma now.'

Perhaps Louise had paid us one last visit I thought. I hoped so.

We slept fitfully on that terrible night to be woken in the morning by Barney dressed in his football kit and asking for a lift to the local high school where he was due to take part in soccer school. It would have been about 10.15 a.m. as we got ready to take him and then drive the two hundred yards from the school to the hospice to see Louise. We had not received the expected phone call in the night and I began to hope against hope that she might be conscious again. We got into the car and as Judy put it into reverse Sam appeared at the front door indicating that there was a phone call. At first we were inclined to leave it, to continue our journey. It would only be someone asking how Louise was, I thought. My instincts, though, said otherwise. I got out of the car and picked up the receiver.

'Hello, Philip, it's Beryl here.'

Beryl Head was the Matron at Trinity.

'We're just on our way,' I replied anxiously.

'I'm sorry Philip, Louise passed away just a few minutes ago. Her Nan was with her.'

I can't remember what I said, but I was suddenly conscious of Judy, Sam and Barney standing beside me. I put the phone down. They already knew from my tone or from what I had said that Louise had died.

'It's over,' I said. I was numb, shocked and I felt physically sick. 'It's finally over.'

I stumbled into the kitchen. Judy walked into the living room and began to cry. Sam went up to his room to hide his grief, to cry in private. Poor Barney followed his mother into the living room and lay underneath the dining room table. He was due to celebrate his tenth birthday in five days time and he had experienced more grief in those ten years than many people experience in a lifetime. I didn't cry, I couldn't, tears wouldn't come. I just stood and felt a huge tide of pain move from my stomach to my heart. My heart began literally to ache and I couldn't breathe properly. The doorbell rang and David Cooper and Beryl Head arrived looking sombre and bearing flowers. I showed them into the living room. The telephone rang, it was a good friend from the local paper enquiring about how Louise was getting on.

'She's dead, Jo,' I said. 'She died at twenty past ten this morning.'

There was a long silence. Jo Biddle had got to know Louise very well during the last year.

'How are you feeling, Philip?'

Her voice was almost a whisper, she sounded embarrassed and upset. I told her that I wasn't feeling anything, although the pain in my heart was becoming much worse.

As news of her passing spread, so the telephone began to ring and by the afternoon the living room was full of flowers. People came and went, many had the red eyes of real grief, but none embarrassed us nor made us feel uncomfortable. An atmosphere of peace seemed to descend upon the house on that awful day. The flowers looked beautiful and really did make a difference. Although we were hurting grievously there was a small element of relief in our bereavement. I don't know for how much longer we could have continued to function as Louise hovered between life and death.

I walked to the shop in the late afternoon sunshine, a walk we had made together so many times. I began to cry quietly as I contemplated our terrible loss. In the newsagent's I could just make out the headline of the local paper through a haze of tears. The huge black letters said it all: Death of a Fighter. And alongside, a beautiful picture of her taken the day before she went to Leeds University. The newsagent stood behind the counter with his head bowed.

'I'm sorry, Philip, I'm so sorry, she was so special.'

'I know,' I said, and I walked out into the bright sun to face a very uncertain and painful future without her.

★

I was awoken from a drug induced sleep the following morning by a loud crash that seemed to come from the porch downstairs. It took a while before I was able to gather my senses and my first thoughts were with Louise. I told myself over and over that she really was dead, that I hadn't been dreaming. As I put on my dressing gown I felt the pain in my heart begin to return. I walked downstairs wearily, leaving Judy lying fully awake staring at the ceiling. I had no doubt that she too was trying to come to terms with that which was not possible ever to come to terms with.

Once downstairs I lit the first cigarette of the day and went to investigate, to see just what had caused the three great thuds. I fully expected to find that the ceiling had collapsed but I didn't care. I opened the door and couldn't believe my eyes, the porch floor was strewn with envelopes and packages, there must have been a hundred or more. I gathered an armful and went upstairs to Judy.

'Have you seen this lot?' I said. 'There are as many again downstairs.'

I went down again to bring up the rest. We spent the next hour or so sitting in bed like two children opening presents on Christmas morning. Nearly every envelope contained a donation to our charity. Every letter expressed great sadness at hearing of Louise's death. And some told a story of personal tragedy and loss. We felt humbled by these amazing gestures of love and goodwill, but more importantly, we knew we were not alone in our pain and grief.

The next morning and the morning after we were awoken by the same crashing thuds in the porch. Amongst the second delivery was a Telemessage from HRH The Princess of Wales, it read:

My thoughts and prayers are with you at this sad and very difficult time. I was so pleased to see Louise last week and admired her strength and courage enormously.

Diana

In total, more than five hundred people wrote to us from all parts of the country. Louise's death had been reported in almost all of the national newspapers, and as the mail and donations piled up we slowly realised just what an inspiration her short life had been to so many others and, more poignantly, just how loved she had been. The week following her death was a very strange and difficult time. Many people visited and some looked as devastated as we were. Chris remained in shock throughout the whole week. He didn't say much. Whenever we spoke he just shook his head in disbelief. Unlike me he had held out hope to the end. He simply hadn't prepared for this at all. We spent a lot of that time arranging Louise's funeral which was to take place exactly a week after her death. Fred visited frequently, to try to ascertain fine detail. He was meticulous in his preparations. This was no ordinary funeral for Fred was going to be burying a very special friend that day.

*

Tuesday 11 August, 1992 dawned bright and wet. I stood staring out of the patio window watching the dripping leaves. The aching in my heart had intensified but I felt far away from tears. It was about 9 a.m. and Louise's funeral was to be held at 11 a.m. Doreen had travelled up from London and I think we were reminiscing about Louise as friends began to arrive and every now and again the telephone rang. Nobody said much as we waited for the arrival of the cars. Mick was, as usual, going to lend us his Bentley and a driver. I remember thinking, as I waited for the cars, that I didn't want it to rain. For some reason I wanted the sun to shine on her coffin, I didn't want it to be muddy.

As we climbed into the Bentley the clouds looked ominously threatening. It was just as if we were going to see the Princess all over again except that there was no joy in any of this, just a relentless aching grief. I put on my sunglasses as the car moved away. I didn't want anyone to see my pain, this was mine and mine alone. I remember noticing as the car cruised slowly behind Louise's hearse, that as we approached the church there were lots of police *no parking* cones. In a flash it occurred to me that there were going to be a lot of people at St John's Church that morning, but even I was shocked as the car turned into the driveway of the church. There were people everywhere. The church seemed to be overflowing. People were lining the drive, standing between the graves, talking in groups. But as we drove to the church they began to look. The talking stopped as we got out of the car, people began to look at us or at least I imagined that they did. I recognised some of the faces in the vast crowd, and as I walked towards the church handshakes and looks of pity greeted me.

Fred came out of church to greet me in full priest regalia. He was smiling sadly.

'Pheel, how are you? Where is Judy?'

I turned to see that Judy was still sitting in the back of the Bentley looking waxen white behind her sunglasses.

'I can't come out Philip,' she said. 'There are too many people, I can't go through with this.'

The boys were sitting beside her looking close to tears.

'Come on Judy, think of Louise, she always faced her crowds. What would she do? Come on, these people are here because they care.'

There was a pleading in my voice and Judy responded.

We walked slowly behind her coffin as it was carried into the dark cool church. There was a strong smell of incense as the gentle music of *Tubular Bells* wafted across the pews. People remained completely silent as we approached the altar. Louise's coffin was placed on a stand before the altar and we took our places at the front beside her.

Once inside I felt safe from the looks and sympathy. It was quiet and peaceful in the church. Judy and the boys just stared ahead as the incense drifted across the altar. I could hear the people behind shuffling into the pews and then everybody fell silent as Fred moved to the lectern. The service was very beautiful. Fred captured the essence of Louise perfectly. All the while I stared at her coffin. I had dreaded this day for so long. I had pictured this image a thousand times, and here I was. The awful nightmare was finally reality; she was gone for ever and I was bereft. I listened to the rain patter insistently on the church roof. Thank you God, I thought thanks a lot.

As we filed out behind the coffin I realised that the church was full to overflowing and that many people who had played a part in this tragically brief life were there. I recognised the deputations from Christie Hospital and Trinity Hospice and noticed people who had been ardent fund-raisers. There were journalists, cab drivers, university students, presenters from the radio station and many ordinary people who had supported our cause anonymously, all weeping and grieving together. She had touched so many lives, and now we were on our way to bury her.

We emerged into bright sunlight. The rain had stopped and the grass glistened. We moved slowly along the path to the end of the graveyard. Under the trees at the far end was a pile of wet clay. Only eight days before I had stood there with Fred as if in a dream on that dark and stormy night. Now we stood watching as our beautiful child was slowly lowered into a dark, damp hole in the ground. Judy began to sob. Barney and Sam began to cry. Fred passed a bowl of holy water and I sprinkled some small drops on to her coffin. My heart continued to ache but I was unable to summon tears. I looked up at the throng all around, they returned my look with piteous looks of their own. So this is what the dreaded end is like, I thought, as I watched five priests offer final ministrations to my daughter. Today had been the stuff of a hundred nightmares, and now it was finally happening I felt detached like an observer at some macabre ritual, unable to intervene yet compelled to watch.

It was a long walk back along the path to the church and the sanctuary of the car. Every so often I heard a mumbled condolence and once or twice people emerged from the crowd to offer their hand or their sympathy. I noticed that they all looked shocked as if this shouldn't be happening. The churchyard was packed with people peering, all seemingly trying to gain an insight into what we were feeling. The looks all said the same thing – how on earth are they going to survive this?

As we climbed into the car I noticed that Judy and the boys

were shaking with emotion. I felt glad that it was all over but terribly unsure of just how I was going to cope without her. I looked out of the car window as we drove through the church gates. The crowd was dispersing now and the gravedigger was enthusiastically and with indecent haste digging at the pile of clay and filling the grave. My stomach tightened with anger and for the first time that day I felt tears trickle down my cheeks as my heart began to break.

I awoke early the following morning. The house was full of the scent of flowers. They were everywhere. In storage jars, cookie jars and borrowed vases. It was a bright late summer morning and I was still feeling distant and detached from the events of the last few weeks. All of my thoughts, though, centred around Louise. Wherever I went in the house there was something of her, but most especially in her room where I felt her presence very powerfully. As I stood staring out of her bedroom window I saw David Cooper's Land Rover pull up outside the house. He had been unable to attend the funeral but had arranged to visit Louise's grave with me that morning. I remember feeling pleased at the thought of returning to her grave, I wanted to be physically close to her. I had spent the night in fitful sleep worrying and fretting about her being all alone in that dark place. I wanted to go to her.

We parked where the hearse had parked the previous day and walked in silence beneath the gently swaying trees to the mound of clay and flowers that was her grave. David stood in silence with his head bowed whilst I knelt beside her grave reading and re-reading the cards and messages. I found the experience deeply moving for as I read each message I pictured a person or an incident or a kind gesture. Everyone had their own fond memories of Louise. Each had seen a facet or glimpse of her personality and character, and some had experienced her love. As I rummaged down amongst the flowers I felt a hard object buried in one of the bouquets at the head of the grave. Hidden within the flowers was a small bottle of diamond white cider from the girls at Leeds University. I felt my eyes smart as I recalled the excited phone calls, 'Daddy, it's wonderful here...' I could almost hear her voice.

We went into the empty church to sit and contemplate. I sat quietly in the front pew that I had occupied the day before. I tried to pray but I couldn't, I was still numb, and I think probably too angry. We climbed back into the Land Rover in silence and drove down the drive towards the main road. As we passed Louise's grave the engine cut out. There was no juddering or spluttering, no warning whatsoever. One minute we were smoothly cruising along in second gear and then, as soon as we came alongside the grave, nothing. David looked shocked, he had owned Land Rovers for decades quite simply because of their reliability. This one was brand new, this was unheard of, everything had simply gone dead.

'Come on Louise,' I said, 'we've got to get home.' David sat beside me looking puzzled. 'Turn the key, David, it'll start now,' I said with complete confidence.

He complied with my request and the engine fired into life. He never had a problem with that car again.

Chapter Ten

And so the days drifted by and almost seemed to merge into one. I began to drink and smoke a lot more than was good for me. Sometimes I caught Fred looking at me with concern and when I caught his glance he always smiled, 'Oh, Pheel,' he'd say, 'you don't need that stuff.'

He was wrong. Of course I needed it. Alcohol diminished pain and enabled sleep. Okay so I had stopped shaving and eating properly, but that was a small price to pay for wonderful moments of oblivion. I began to spend long periods by her grave. Just sitting on a small wooden bench completely in a world of my own. Days came and went and still I sat there completely absorbed by my loss. I didn't want to do anything else. A friend who had lost his eleven-year-old child to cancer had recently been admitted to the local psychiatric unit. Compared to him, I reasoned, I was doing well.

When I wasn't at the grave I was in the pub. I began to meet Chris regularly at her grave and then we would walk into Poulton together to sit by the fire in the pub and drink large whiskies and pints of beer. We didn't really talk much. Chris read his *Sporting Life* and I stared into the fire and let the alcohol do its work. I enjoyed those times because I couldn't face reality. Reality was getting myself back to work and trying to come to terms with this grievous loss and I didn't want any of that.

One afternoon I was in the supermarket with Judy and I saw my reflection in the window. I looked terrible, unshaven and tired, but more importantly I noticed that I looked like a frightened animal. I was all hunched up. Shoulders high, arms folded. It was almost as if I was turning in on myself, holding myself for comfort, hunched against the world outside. For a brief moment I was alarmed and just as quickly I didn't care once more.

As soon as we returned home that day the telephone rang. It

was just twenty days since Louise's death and it was a day that I shall never forget.

'Mr Woolcock?'

'Yes?' I snapped.

'It's *The Sun* newspaper here. Are you aware that the Princess of Wales has flown from Balmoral to Blackpool? She's waiting for you at Trinity Hospice.'

I told the reporter that I had lost my daughter recently and that I thought his joke was in poor taste. I hung up. As soon as I put the receiver down the phone rang again.

'Mr Woolcock? It's the *Daily Express* here...'

The same story. I was incredulous. Four more newspapers phoned in the space of as many minutes. I had had enough, I telephoned the hospice. David Cooper sounded tense and anxious.

'Where on earth have you been? I've been trying to phone you all afternoon. Diana's here, she's waiting to see you both now. Bring the boys.'

Judy went into a panic.

'I need a shower,' she said, 'and just look at the state you're in!'

I looked in the mirror; she was right, I looked as if I had slept rough for a week. Before I knew it the boys were washed and changed, Judy showered and I was standing in front of the bathroom mirror removing five days stubble. Within twenty minutes we were on our way to Trinity. I was transformed, clean-shaven and smartly suited.

As we approached the hospice we were flagged down by a police officer and asked our identity. I think he was expecting us for we were directed into the car park immediately. As we got out of the car flash bulbs began to explode from our left. I noticed a huddle of reporters and photographers being kept back by one or two policemen from the hospice entrance. There was an atmosphere of tension and expectancy as we walked into reception. David was with us immediately.

'You'll meet her in a small side room, follow me.'

We duly followed David along the corridor until we reached a side door. He opened the door and ushered us inside. It was a small room, about twelve feet square, with a small settee, some chairs and a coffee table. It was the sort of room people receive bad news in, and I remember wondering just how many people had been ushered into this room to be told that loved ones had died. I was contemplating these thoughts when the door opened and Diana walked in closely followed by David Cooper.

'Shall I stay?' he asked hesitantly, as Diana sat opposite me.

'No, I'd rather you left us alone,' she replied.

David left, and once again we were alone with the Princess of Wales. This time things were very different.

'I'm so sorry,' she said, 'Louise was a very brave young woman, you should be very proud of her. She achieved so much.'

Diana seemed genuinely moved as she spoke. Barney and Sam were sitting on the small settee to her right. She asked them their names and they looked awe struck. She made some small talk with the boys before returning to talk about Louise. She asked us how we were coping, about our anger and our pain, and all the while her eyes were boring deep, sensing and reaching out as if she was trying to feel our pain.

She was wearing a dark blue two piece suit, and yet again I found myself drawn to her physical presence. She was tanned, lean and radiated good health. Her hair shone and bounced as she spoke and her eyes sparkled. And then they sparkled too much. There were tears forming in her eyes as she spoke. She had switched the conversation from Louise and was now talking about the media. Her hands had formed tight fists on her lap and her knuckles were bright white. I was suddenly aware of her tension.

'The problem is that I can't answer back, I have no right of reply,' she said, her voice rising slightly, and she began to sound annoyed. She was talking about some tapes that had been sold to a tabloid newspaper. 'It was my voice on those tapes, Philip. That's not a conversation I've had; they've doctored the tape, but no one will listen. I just have to sit and take it.' And then the bombshell was dropped almost casually into the conversation as her anger rose and her eyes filled with tears. 'I've had eleven years of this crap and I'm getting out.'

She looked across the table into my eyes. She was almost pleading.

'Nobody should have to put up with all this, I've had enough.'

I couldn't believe my ears. The Princess of Wales was telling me that her marriage was over. What could I say? She began to talk quickly and I noticed that she was shaking slightly. My heart went out to her. I mumbled some words of comfort. I told her that the Duchess of York got a worse press. I told her how loved she was and how important she had become to us. I moved the conversation back to Louise.

'You were an inspiration to her,' I said. 'You must carry on.'

She was calmer now and seemed pleased with my response. The conversation turned once more to Louise and she asked what practical things we were doing to manage our grief from day to day. Judy talked of her responsibilities to, and love for, Sam and Barney. Diana visibly brightened and talked of her own boys. Sam and Barney looked slightly embarrassed as Diana and Judy became quite animated, comparing notes concerning their priceless boys. I began to sense that it was almost time for this encounter to end. Diana turned to me and said, 'And how do you cope with your loss, Philip?'

She was earnest in her enquiry as she fixed her eyes on mine. I told her the truth.

'I don't really,' I replied. 'I sometimes write things down. Just thoughts and memories,' I said casually. I remembered that I had written a poem about Louise some days before and I had hurriedly put it into my jacket as I left the house because I felt that it explained a lot of what I was feeling. I passed it to her. Diana read the poem slowly and carefully.

'It's beautiful,' she said. 'You should write everything down, I'm sure it will help you a lot, Philip.' She was becoming quite enthusiastic now. 'You must write about Louise and your feelings. You write so beautifully. Louise's story should be told.'

Her eyes were bright again and I was transfixed by her enthusiasm. She asked if she could keep the poem that I had written. Naturally I was pleased to let her have it.

'Send me your writing, Philip, I'll be pleased to read it. I promise it will help you feel better.'

There was a gentle knock and David Cooper put his head around the door. The meeting was about to end, her car was now ready to go. I felt that she wanted to stay, to talk more, to know more about Louise and our long battle with cancer. Unfortunately, she was booked onto a scheduled flight back to Balmoral, and she expressed concern that the flight would not wait for her! She shook hands with Sam and Barney and then with Judy and myself.

'Keep writing, Philip,' she said, 'and don't forget you have your boys, Judy.'

She left then and once again we were left dumbstruck. The future Queen of England had just told us she was going to be divorced. She had confided her most intimate secrets to us. No sooner had she left us than she was whisked away, once again, in the green Jaguar.

She was very unhappy that day and as we left the hospice a few minutes after her we got a taste of what it was like to be Diana Princess of Wales. At first it was the exploding flashlights and then the jostling. 'What did she say?'

They all seemed to be shouting at once as microphones were thrust beneath my nose. 'Tell us about your friendship with the Princess, Mr Woolcock.'

'What did she say about Louise?'

At one point I feared for the safety of Sam and Barney as the massed ranks of paparazzi pushed relentlessly forward. I spoke only of my daughter's illness and of our bereavement but they wanted more, much more, I was very conscious that any comments regarding our recent conversation would cause uproar in the press, and I persisted with my mundane answers – I owed Diana at least that much.

We arrived home in shock. First we tried to take in the very private conversation we had just had. But more than that was the overwhelming sympathy we felt for this young woman who, day in, day out, had to live her life with all its ups and downs in this very public way. We had just had a small taste of this and it had left us emotionally exhausted and desperate for the sanctuary of our beloved home. Once there, we tried to comprehend what it must be like to live such a life. I had found the press to be intimidating and quite threatening in their desire to get a story. It seemed to me that had I given them the merest hint of a story, or better still a scandal, I would have been hounded and harassed until they had what they wanted. I shuddered to think of what this young woman must have gone through, especially in the early years of her fame when she was wholly unused to such attention. No wonder she was so upset, I thought, no wonder she was getting out after eleven years. I began to see how lucky we were in our anonymity. I changed back into my jeans, lit a cigarette and thought about why she had come. Ten minutes later I found myself sitting beside Louise's grave telling her about Diana's third visit.

When I arrived home about an hour later Judy had taken a number of calls from the press who had, I think, still sensed there was a story in our meeting with Diana. She stuck to her guns and told them we had discussed only our daughter and our feelings concerning our loss. I was pleased with our stance, for I felt that Diana had been betrayed quite enough. For the rest of that day I was plagued by the image of the Princess of Wales, frustrated, almost pleading and desperately unhappy. In spite of all this she had come to the hospice – or was it because of all this?

It would have been about 8 p.m. on the day following her visit that the phone rang. I was sitting on the patio in the fading light thinking about that stormy night just before Louise died. It was calm now and the heady perfume of night scented stocks was evoking, yet again, powerful memories of happy times spent with goblins and pixies. At first I ignored the incessant ringing hoping it would go away. Finally out of irritation I felt compelled to answer.

'Yes!' I snapped as I picked up the receiver.

'Could I speak to Philip Woolcock, please?'

The voice was unmistakable. I faltered in my reply; it can't be, I thought. It was.

'Is it convenient to talk, Philip?' she said and sounded almost apologetic.

She thanked me for our kindness the day before and hoped we hadn't minded being burdened with her problems then thanked me for the beautiful poem I had given her. There was a pause and then she apologised for us being hounded by the press.

'I was so pleased you didn't speak to them, Philip,' she said. 'I half expected to see our conversation all over the tabloids.'

She sounded genuinely grateful and, as usual, completely

devoid of airs and graces. She asked after Judy and the boys and then reminded me that I had promised her that I would try to express my pain through writing.

'It's a wonderful story, Philip. It should be written. Apart from anything else it will make you feel so much better.'

She sounded keen that I should express my pain in this way. I promised that I would write, but in my heart of hearts I didn't even feel much like speaking at that time. I hadn't properly grieved yet. I was afraid that if I cried I would never stop.

★

As the summer turned to autumn I found myself more and more drawn to the churchyard, to her settling grave. I sat there for hours deep in thought. Flowers rotted and early autumn wasps hovered and hummed amongst the debris of stalks, ribbons and rain soaked cards. Sometimes I spoke to her, but mostly I just relived memory after memory. The unforgettable days her brothers were born. She always clung closer then. Times when it snowed, tiny cold pink hands forming icy snowballs, her face a picture of rapt concentration. Blonde curls tumbling over her grey duffle coat. Dancing and kicking swathes of crisp yellow leaves, laughing without any trace of inhibition. And of course hot summer evenings spent in another world. I too began to lose my sense of reality. I was easily transported by those powerful memories and quickly became irritated when the real world had the audacity to intrude.

Then one early October morning I was sitting, as usual, by her grave and I felt an overwhelming urge to write something down. It was almost as if Louise was standing next to me. I felt her presence so strongly.

'Come on, Daddy, it's time to do it now.'

As she spoke to me a shaft of sunlight rested on the grave and I knew that I had to start writing, I went home and wrote the following piece:

We buried Louise on a bright morning six weeks ago. It was just two years and eleven months since we were told that she would not recover from her cancer – two years and eleven months of pain, anger, sadness and great joy – a period of immense anguish, an unforgettable odyssey into the unknown. She was just twenty-one years old. There is no doubt that our daughter was exceptional, not just as a scholar (she was mediocre in some disciplines) or a heroine (she was very frightened in the end), but a spirit with a huge capacity to inspire and to give love. She was blessed with a strange kind of brightness, an inner light, and this more than anything, enabled those around her to find their own strength and to come to terms with their human frailties. She was certainly inspirational.

Throughout her illness she refused to give in to the lurking parasite that was eventually to, so horribly, destroy her body, but which failed to touch her spirit. When she lost her beautiful tangled hair she cried and shouted and then refused to wear a wig or a headscarf. She pitied those who stared, she never felt different or ugly (in fact, she became even more beautiful). During chemotherapy, as she became violently and sometimes uncontrollably sick, she would swear vociferously in between her 'contractions' and then, breathing heavily, she would smile pale and shaking and with her eyes full of the tears of sheer physical exertion, she would ask for a chopped egg or whatever strange food had taken her fancy.

Eventually, we became used to her body-breaking regime of poison, nausea, partial recovery, and those heart rending Monday mornings when she had to return to Christie, every third week, to be subjected to her 'torture.' In between we spent indescribably precious times together. Hanging on my arm she'd struggle to the pub for a half of Guinness or wander aimlessly around shops to buy trinkets, tapes or outrageous clothes. Sometimes we would sit together in her room (now something of a shrine) whilst she painted her nails bright orange or yellow or applied the most garish lipstick. Always the brightest colours. She was always striking, vivid and self-willed. Always tactile and loquacious. We would talk for hours and then a long bony hug would end with her exclaiming 'Oh, Daddy!' as if I were a simpleton, someone to be pitied. I often left the room wondering just what I'd said, or done to deserve this declamation. Or was it a cry of love?

She was determined to take her place at Leeds University and as September last year approached we became increasingly *apprehensive. Eighteen months intensive treatment was now over, she was stronger, her cropped hair and red Doc Martens made her look normal and we had to keep convincing ourselves that she wasn't, that she was, in fact, dying of cancer – that this was just remission, a cruel, malicious mirage.*

We packed her belongings and drove her to Leeds. She was resolute in her determination to get there. We took her to her bare tiny room in the hall of residence and I begged her to return home with us. I longed to nurse her again. But no, she was independent now and this heady drug had seduced her completely. 'Daddy, it's beautiful,' she cried.

We walked quietly back to the car, past weeping parents who were leaving their sons and daughters for the first time. I too was crying – crying with anger.

When we visited Louise about a fortnight later her room had been transformed with posters, books, tapes and lots of bright colours. She had been elected by her fellow students to represent them on some university committee. She was as happy as I had ever seen her. She was bubbly, bright and enthusiastic. She talked non-stop of her new life, of the drinking, the concerts, and the late nights. Just two weeks later she returned home for a planned weekend with one of her new friends and told us how she had found a new lump in her groin. We froze, we knew this was the beginning of the end: her cancer was active again. She spent the next two weeks in Christie having further tests and treatment; determined throughout to return to Leeds, to her freedom, her independence.

We had a wonderful last Christmas together (we always had wonderful Christmases). My attempts to persuade her not to return to Leeds failed as usual, and as I tearfully loaded her possessions into a taxi I knew she'd be back. During that spring term Louise was ecstatically happy. Joyous phone calls, wonderful exam results – she came head of the whole year. Then shortly after her Easter break, a change of tone, 'Mummy, I'm tired, I want to come home.'

The next day she arrived pale and worried, so obviously dis-tressed and in pain. We telephoned Christie and after a weekend of worry she was admitted for tests. The following Thursday she was told that her cancer had spread and that she was dying. We thought she might have had twelve months. Louise was stoical behind her tears but frightened and very angry. Her demise accelerated, pain control became difficult. Friends visited and were visibly shocked by her rapid deterioration. Morphine was administered in increasingly large doses. She lost weight and cried out in the night in anger and fear. Eventually she agreed to being admitted to our hospice. By this time she was drifting in and out of consciousness. She spent two weeks in their love and expert care and then characteristically demanded to come home.

The next six days were like a dreadful nightmare; support services were superb. Oh, but the desperate cries of anguish and unadulterated terror was sometimes just too much to bear. There were short, more lucid periods when she seemed to be at peace and during one of these she asked to be anointed into the Catholic Church. The priest (our friend) was summoned and held her hand, or what was left of it. It was a short, very moving service, after which Louise turned smiling to Fred and told him that she loved him and that she would pray for him. I shall never forget the look of love and peace on her face at that precious moment. Two days later she returned to the hospice at her own request.

'I'll be back, Daddy,' she said. The following morning she died.

Louise has left an indelible mark upon us all. Her special light lives on in our hearts, although the pain of the loss is sometimes unbearable. For two years and eleven months we shared everything. We laughed, we cried, we talked. Every moment was precious and unforgettable. We have all absorbed some of that special spirit and are so much stronger for that experience. Today as I stood by her grave the sun broke through the heavy grey cloud and I'm sure I heard her laughter.

I sent this piece to Diana, as I had promised.

Friends told me later that during the twelve months following Louise's death my body language became distinctive. When walking I would hunch up excessively, arms pressed tight into my sides and hands thrust deep into my pockets. I became short with people and introverted. I even had a corner of the kitchen in which I sat for hours alone, drinking, smoking and thinking. I resented intrusion during these times.

A few months after Louise died Judy went to work as a school secretary. My job as a child care manager had long since been re-distributed, given my long absence, and I was offered work with the elderly and dying. Even my GP was appalled by their apparent insensitivity, and I resigned in April 1993 having collected a few months pay. At that time I didn't want to work, I didn't see the point.

That year saw me becoming increasingly absorbed by my loss. I went to her grave every day, touched her gravestone, talked to her incessantly, but usually I just sat on the bench, sometimes with Uncle Chris, but mostly alone. Judy became worried by my behaviour. One day a Macmillan nurse we knew called at the school where Judy worked and, in passing, asked how we were getting on. Judy told the nurse of her concerns about my mental state and she came straight round to see me. Mel looked shocked when I reluctantly answered the door. I had been drinking already that day and probably hadn't shaved. Mel asked me lots of questions about my feelings, but I wasn't really interested in giving proper answers. In fact, I recall, in horror now, that I was very rude to her. I told her that her job was futile, that she was wasting her time. I assured her that I was perfectly well and would be much better occupied doing anything other than having this conversation. She left, but not before she told me that she thought I was suffering from depression and that she would arrange for me to have counselling at the hospice. With hindsight her intervention came too late. This visit took place almost a year after Louise's death.

I went for one or possibly two sessions with David Cooper. It was pointless, with the greatest respect to him. We simply chatted about Louise and what had become my obsession with her death; anger didn't come into the equation, and it was anger that I was feeling and failing to express.

As the first anniversary of her death approached so Fred came more into the picture.

'Pheel, you're drinking too much, you're behaving badly. This isn't what Louise would have wanted.'

He began to confront what he perceived, rightly or wrongly, as my self-destructive urges. Sometimes he became angry, at other times he just looked at me with pity and fear in his eyes. Something had to give, and in October 1993 I left home. I was offering my family nothing. I had become absorbed in my own pain. I moved in with Fred, Father Muir and Father Joseph at St John's Presbytery.

Fred was adamant that I should confront my unacceptable behaviour and begin to look towards the future. All three priests seemed to take it in turns to work on me. Fred woke me at dawn and insisted I get out of bed. Father Muir tempted me into the lounge after dinner with large whiskies and cigarettes and Joseph (newly-arrived from Uganda) invited me into his kitchen to watch him cook exotic African stews. All the while Fred busied himself as a go-between, always driving to see Judy and the boys, and returning to me to tell me how much I was needed. I began to drink less, to sleep without temazepam, I even started to think about going to work. My reflections, although still painful, seemed to focus more on the positive aspects of that terrible journey, and less upon my tremendous loss. Of course, I hurt like hell at times, but there were other times when I reflected with a smile on the great good that came from it all. The pain eased into a yearning, a longing for her laugh, her temper tantrums and her arm upon mine. Throughout all this time my anger slowly subsided and I began to think that I could, after all, make a go of things at home.

The clincher came one late October night whilst smoking a last cigarette. The phone rang and I was loathed to answer. Fred and Joseph were out and Father Muir had long since gone to bed. Nobody ever phoned me there and I had visions of answering the phone to a potential suicide who was intent on having a last confession. Nevertheless, I answered in trepidation, determined to let the caller know as quickly as possible that I wasn't a priest. The voice had now become all too familiar.

'Could I speak to Philip Woolcock, please?'

I had no idea at first how she knew I was there nor how she got the number. But as she spoke it dawned upon me that my departure from home had been heralded in a headline in the local paper: Louise's Parents in Split, a pointless story really, but somehow she had got wind of it.

'Is it convenient to talk, Philip?'

Her manners were, as ever, impeccable. Diana expressed her sadness at hearing of our separation. She asked me of the effects on the boys and then talked of such things being common following bereavement, especially following the loss of a child. She spoke of her work with Relate, and of how things would work themselves out. Most importantly, Diana talked of what a tough team Judy and I were; how, when she had met us, she had sensed our closeness. In the end she advised me to go home to where I belonged and to start again. Sadly, Diana talked of her own loss in marriage and of how much her boys needed their father.

'Your boys have been hurt enough, Philip, can't you see that?'

I could, and the following day I went home and began to contemplate a future for the first time in four years. Diana had stepped into our lives yet again, but this time she offered hope instead of sympathy.

Chapter Eleven

Later that week I made a very important decision. I decided to return to teaching. I had left teaching for social work almost ten years before and had, for some time, contemplated a return to the classroom. Holidays and hours were certainly an attraction but, more importantly, it was something that I felt I could do well. I registered as a supply teacher at the local education office and waited for the phone to ring. The calls soon came and I did a day here and a day there, but I needed the chance to do some longer term work to see if it was really for me. The chance came unexpectedly. I had worked for almost a week at a local High School in south Blackpool. I knew that the Deputy Head had been impressed by my performance because he had told me so. He felt that I had 'a way with children', especially the more difficult ones.

*

It was just before Christmas 1993 and I had settled well at home. The Deputy Head asked me to come to his office. The head of special needs was due to leave in a week's time; the school had not found a suitable replacement, would I like to take over in the New Year for a couple of terms just to see how things went? I didn't hesitate. It wasn't just the money, I had actually begun to enjoy my work. Of course I would do it!

We spent a very quiet Christmas at home as I prepared for a new start in the new year. I spent a lot of time at Louise's grave and even more time with Uncle Chris. Before I knew it, it was time to start the new term. I clearly remember the night before. The following day I was to begin work as Head of a large department, but moreover as tutor to a form of year ten students who had a certain reputation. I was scared. I had been away from this sort of reality for over four years, I had been living in a very different world. I felt as a soldier returning from a bloody war might feel. I recall sitting alone on that night unable to sleep, thoroughly convinced that I would fail. I hadn't taught for so long. What if I froze? What if the children just laughed at me? I had a quiet conversation with Louise.

'Come on,' I whispered, 'you help me, you'd know what to do.'

I imagined her reply.

'Oh, Daddy stop being such an arse, you'll do it standing on your head!'

Thinking of her, of what she went through and the way she coped, put my imagined difficulties into perspective – of course I would cope. How could I fail? I'd just been to hell and back what could a bunch of kids do to me?

As I walked along the corridor towards my form room my confidence began to evaporate. It was just too quiet, perhaps 10L2 had got the date wrong, perhaps they were all still at home tucked up in bed, perhaps I had got the date wrong. Maybe I shouldn't be here until tomorrow; unfortunately, nobody had got the date wrong. I walked through the door and was closely examined by twenty-five surly-looking fifteen year olds. The atmosphere was electric, the teacher in me kicked in instinctively.

'Good morning, 10L2,' I roared with total confidence.

It worked, the tension level dropped. There was an uncoordinated mumbling.

'Good morning, sir,' they replied reluctantly.

And then the unthinkable happened, my taking of the register was interrupted by a large and menacing-looking boy at the back of the room who had decided to instigate a conversation, not with his neighbour, but with another boy at the other side of the room. The gauntlet had been thrown down, I had to respond. I removed my spectacles meaningfully and placed my pen on the table in the manner of a confident card shark. The silence was palpable, the atmosphere tense. I fixed the transgressor in my sights and slowly walked towards him.

'Do you have a problem with silence?' My voice had become a whisper now I was angry.

'No.'

'Pardon?' I whispered.

I could see that he was desperately trying to weigh me up to see if a victory was possible.

'No sir,' he said.

I had won, Gavin Bradley had backed down and my reputation was secured.

I spent a wonderful two terms at that school. 10L2 became known as Mr Woolcock's posse. My tutorial sessions became the stuff of legend. Naturally I talked to them about Louise. Many of the children knew who I was from publicity in the local paper. They sat entranced as I spoke of her courage and of her fears. I always brought her short life and struggle into the context of their own lives. A theme for a tutorial might be 'the nature of courage' or 'coping in adversity'. Her life began to become a shining example to young people, many of whom were confused or unhappy as only fifteen years olds can be. The children threw themselves into raising funds for our charity, and by the time I left in July 1994 the whole school had got behind me in my efforts to continue to fund our day hospice.

The day after I left that school I visited Louise's grave. It was a beautiful warm late July morning and as I walked down the path to her grave I noticed that in addition to flowers that we left each week, there were more lying flat on the grass with a card attached. The card read, 'For Louise, thanks for everything, from the posse'. Yes, Louise, I thought, thanks for everything. I had made a more than successful return to teaching and she had given me the confidence to do that. She had been there for me throughout. And what of Gavin Bradley? Well, he cried when I left. But more importantly he phoned me the other week; he's nearly twenty now.

In September 1994 I moved to a twelve month contract at Louise's old school in Blackpool. At that time I didn't want, or indeed need, the security of a permanent contract with all the attendant commitment. I continued to move from school to school, from contract to contract I enjoyed my return to teaching and I was happy. Quite recently I did finally apply for what Judy calls a 'proper job' and am now working at a local High School as a head of department – permanently!

Diana never lost touch. In fact, she became even closer. Just before Christmas 1995, two years after her last call, she telephoned us to see how we were doing. She seemed a little down at the time, but we were delighted to hear her voice again. She spoke at length to Judy about the boys and seemed keen to know how Sam and Barney were doing. She talked with me about Louise and I told her of my return to teaching and of how rewarding I had found that experience. She was fascinated when I told her that at times I could feel Louise's presence; often when I was tired or a little despairing. I told Diana of how Louise would sometimes come to me at such moments, of how her presence was almost tangible and of how inspiring she was to me.

'She's watching you, Philip, you can be sure of that,' she said. She sounded certain of this and it seemed to please her. 'And what about the book, Philip?' she sounded like a teacher demanding homework.

'I've done it,' I said, and I had.

I had written almost sixty thousand words between October and December 1993. I told her I wasn't happy with it and we talked about the style and content.

'Do it again,' she said, 'you must write Louise's life, even if you don't publish it. It will be something for your boys. Louise's story should be told.'

Once again she told me it would be of help to others. At the end of that call Diana asked me if we were still running our charity and seemed quite pleased when I told her we had closed a few months earlier.

'It was a magnificent effort, Philip. You should always be proud of that, but you have to get on with your life now, you've done enough for others.'

Diana contacted us again in the Spring of 1996 and, yet again, she spoke to Judy of her boys. It seemed to us that her sons were becoming her *raison d'etre*. She seemed fascinated by our mundane every day lives, and I wondered if this was just part of her charm or was she really interested in our rather boring and sometimes tedious existence?

The following year on Thursday 31 July, 1997 the telephone rang at 8.30pm. I answered the phone fully expecting it to be for one of the boys as it invariably was.

'Hello Philip,' she said bright and bubbly. There was a smile in her voice.

'Is it convenient to talk?'

I felt like telling her that it wasn't, that I was busy making a cup of coffee. Had I said this I am absolutely sure that she would have apologised profusely and offered to phone later. Her humility should never be underestimated, it was one of the reasons she was so able to communicate effectively with ordinary people.

I told her how pleasantly surprised I was to hear from her, and she thanked me for an article I had written and sent to her a day or two before. I told her that she sounded happy and she began to giggle, 'I am, Philip, I'm gloriously happy,' she said.

She asked how we were and I told her that we were as happy as we could be, there were still sometimes bad days when simple things seemed like awful chores.

'Louise was a beacon, Philip, a guiding light for so many, you should always treasure that.'

I told her that I did, but that sometimes living without her was impossibly painful. Diana spoke of how one day she was certain we would be reunited, and in the meantime Louise would always be with me in spirit. She asked me who was looking after me and I told her with genuine cynicism that everybody looks after themselves.

'Everyone needs someone to look after them,' she said, 'even you.'

She giggled infectiously and asked how Judy was.

'She's here if you'd like to ask her.'

Before I passed her to Judy I told her how pleased I was that she seemed to have found some happiness.

Judy loved it when Diana rang. She told Diana about Sam and Barney and how concerned she was that Sam had recently had his navel pierced and a gold ring inserted. Diana laughed with mock horror. 'I don't know what my mother-in-law would say if William did that!'

Judy told her about an incident that had occurred on Louise's birthday six months before. Sam, had taken up residence in

Louise's room, had returned home from a night out at about 2 a.m. He settled into bed and was just falling asleep when his stereo suddenly lit up and began to play music. Simultaneously Louise's posters which had been firmly stuck to the bedroom wall for five years or more, sprang from the wall and onto the bed. Sam is calm by nature, but was shaken by this. He got out of bed, put the posters back on the wall and went back to bed. Ten minutes later the whole scene repeated itself. The stereo came on and the posters leapt from the wall. This time Sam decided enough was enough and Judy found him the next morning fast asleep on Barney's bedroom floor. Diana was fascinated by this tale. She told Judy that Louise was communicating with us and that we must see a psychic. Judy told her that she felt uneasy about doing this as she didn't want to disturb Louise. Diana reassured her that all her friends visited psychics and that it gave our loved ones the chance to let us know that they were all right.

I have to confess that there had been a number of unexplained incidents since Louise's death, and I had sometimes wondered whether she really was trying to get in touch. Sinead O'Connor had written to us shortly before Diana's call saying that Louise had been 'in touch' with her on two occasions since her death.

Diana perhaps spent longer on the phone with Judy than with me. She was excited about her forthcoming trip to Bosnia and, I think, happy in her new relationship. She told Judy she was still being a rebel. Judy laughed and told her Louise would be proud of her; she passed the phone back to me to end the call. Diana said she would be in touch very soon. After that call we sat together in the kitchen and reflected upon the strange and tragic circumstance of our having befriended the Princess of Wales. To this day we will never understand just why she had invested so much in us. What was it about Louise and her plight that had fascinated her so? There had certainly been a strong chemistry between those two young women and I had always meant to ask Diana, why us?

*

On Saturday 2 August, just two days before the fifth anniversary of Louise's death, the doorbell rang. The delivery man was almost hidden behind the basketful of flowers, such was its size. I manoeuvred the flowers into the living room and read the accompanying card. 'I'll be thinking of you on 4 August, with lots of love to you all, Diana'. She had gauged our mood perfectly during that last telephone call. It was a beautiful and thoughtful gesture and the pain of that fifth anniversary was much alleviated by the thought that Diana had entered our lives once again and was, in spite of an engagement in Bosnia, still thinking of us, and of Louise. Upon returning from Louise's grave that day I wrote the following short article for our local newspaper.

> It is exactly five years since Louise died from her cancer. I say her cancer because it was very particular to her. She talked to it, cursed it and tried to destroy it, but in the end it prevailed and won.
>
> Five years is a significant period for victims of this disease. Five years cancer-free, following treatment, is reckoned to be an all-clear, and most people talk in terms of victory and get on with their lives.
>
> In my case, five years has a different meaning. It has been a time of attempting, and failing, to come to terms with a dreadful and irreconcilable loss. A time of pain, great sadness and a terrible longing. A time of waking from fitful sleep with a soul-numbing feeling of disbelief and horror, of nightmares, anger and an indescribable sense of loss.
>
> You may wonder why I did not receive counselling. I have to admit that a few weeks after Louise died I was visited, by chance, by a nurse who immediately realised I needed help. I subsequently attended counselling sessions where I was asked how I felt and how I was spending my time. They offered sympathetic noises but no answers, because there weren't any, and they knew it.
>
> I returned to teaching and I did find some succour. My students showed kindness, sympathy and understanding. Because of the publicity that had surrounded Louise's illness they were aware of who I was and they responded with sensitivity and tact. If any healing has taken place, it has been because of the support I received from these youngsters. Not because of 'time' or 'getting on with my life'.
>
> Time does not heal; it makes things worse. One is conscious only of its passing, of others growing and moving on, of Louise's

fellow university students graduating, getting married or starting work. But, most painfully, of her two brothers growing up without their precious sister, and of wondering just what she would be doing now or how she would have grown herself.

'You've got to get on with your life' – bereaved parents are often told by well meaning people who may have lost a parent or grandparent. Losing a child is different. One feels guilty for being alive. It is a grossly unnatural event. Life after that isn't for getting on with, it is for surviving with a pain that you know will never go away – nor should it.

Today, as always, I spent time at Louise's grave. My thoughts were of the wonderful times we spent together, her marvellous achievements, her laughter and her sheer joie de vivre. I am very proud of the way she dealt with her illness. She never let cancer crush her spirit.

I sometimes wonder if my feelings about this tremendous loss are not 'normal'. Shouldn't I be feeling better? Shouldn't the pain have lessened by now? Am I being self indulgent?

I recently bumped into a man whose young son had died of cancer a year before we lost Louise. Our families had tried to help one another through our respective loss and trauma. Naturally, I asked him how he was feeling. 'Terrible, Philip, bloody terrible,' he said, and he looked it.

On the morning of 31 August, 1997 the phone rang at 5.05 a.m. Our immediate assumption was that something terrible had happened to our son who had not returned home from his Saturday night out.

Judy answered nervously as I stood on the landing. She went quiet for what seemed like an eternity, but in reality was probably only a few seconds, before exclaiming, 'Oh my God, I'll put Philip on.'

I went cold with dread and anticipation as I took the phone from her.

'Diana's dead,' she said. She spoke in a matter of fact way, but looked stunned.

At the other end of the line a young news reporter from the local radio station confirmed Judy's pronouncement. I stood as if in a dream, disbelieving that Diana was ever really mortal – she simply radiated life too beautifully and brightly to ever succumb to anything as shocking and ordinary as death.

The reporter asked me for my reaction on air. At first I told him I didn't have one. I could barely collect my thoughts. He got his soundbite in the end, but I cannot recall what I said. A part of me was speaking, but most of my mind was occupied with thoughts of this extraordinary woman – her hair, her eyes, her laughter, but most of all her glowing radiance, her compassion, her boys and her passionate vocation.

Like everyone else I switched on the TV, still not believing that any of what I had heard could be true. Every few minutes the presenter made the same grim announcement: 'Diana, Princess of Wales was killed this morning...' He spoke as if he could not accept it himself. I occurred to me that Martyn Lewis was in the same state of mind as I was. We were both trying to will ourselves not to believe this terrible news.

As Sunday dawned, appropriately grey and damp, so reality crept slowly in, and I thought of that last phone call just four weeks previously.

'Hello, Philip, is it convenient to talk.'

Always the same introduction, the same exquisite manners and then the giggles – she loved to surprise us and she never failed to do so.

She had sounded so blissfully happy during that last call. I pictured her sitting alone at Kensington Palace, her spirit overflowing with a heady new love of life. I thought of my daughter Louise phoning from university to tell us of her excellent exam results or recalling a particularly wonderful night out. Diana sounded like that. Classical music was playing faintly in the background as she spoke of her forthcoming visit to Bosnia, of her precious boys, and of the impact that Louise had made upon her. After about fifteen minutes she asked to speak to Judy – she always did. Their conversations were somehow different from those which I had with her, perhaps more intimate. With Judy she spoke of our boys always enquiring after their health, their foibles, girlfriends and exploits.

She seemed desperate to know how families functioned outside the limelight, always comparing and contrasting our life with hers, I think she envied much of what we had – especially our privacy, but mostly, I think the fact that we had been so happily married for so long.

'You are such a tough team, Philip, and I so admire you both for that. You have come through so much together.'

She had repeated this during other conversations in far less happy times.

There had indeed been many less happy times. Times when she would pour out her heart in grief over the breakdown of her marriage, and during its terrible aftermath. Times when media intrusion was driving her to distraction.

'Philip, they can say what they like, but how can I ever answer them back? It's so unfair.'

I wanted to answer back for her, but how could I? Even her closest courtiers and friends were accused of manipulation when they rose to her defence. Eventually, she broke and did the *Panorama* interview. It was a mistake, and, although she was supported by opinion polls, I think she knew it.

As I sat in my dressing gown on that dreadful grey morning the phone began to ring. We hurriedly decided that we would give interviews – at last a chance to answer back for her. We subsequently spent the next year appearing in the press, television and radio. We even did three prime time interviews for NBC television in America. I think our decision to talk of our relationship with Diana was justified.

It is now almost two years since her tragic death and I am still trying to come to terms with the fact that I will never see or talk to her again. No more of that infectious laughter, no more silliness and giggles. But more sadly, no more of that feeling of utter helplessness as she poured out her frustration and unhappiness, the victim of both her power and her incredible vulnerability.

I shall never forget the way she came into our lives like an angel of mercy, giving so much and asking nothing in return. Always there for a family who, at the time, were struggling to find some way forward, some meaning following a devastating bereavement. The beautiful basket of flowers that she sent us on the fifth anniversary of Louise's death now sits dried up in the garage as a poignant reminder to us of the brevity of life, the ephemeral nature of beauty.

At night I contemplate the framed photographs of two beautiful young women with so much to offer the world and everything to live for, now both dead. And as I try to come to terms with this grievous loss I clearly recall the prophetic words she spoke to me during our final conversation. We were talking about the death of her friend Gianni Versace and I spoke of having seen photographs of her looking distraught at his funeral. She had sighed so deeply.

'Isn't it awful, Philip, that talented and beautiful people always seem to die so tragically?'

Finally...

This summer we approach the seventh anniversary of Louise's untimely death. In that time the world has become a very different place for us. She still lives each day in our hearts, and not a day goes by when I don't think of her. Sometimes I laugh when I reflect upon her eccentricities or her temper, sometimes I still cry inside and feel the all too familiar pricking in my eyes, but mostly I wonder at her strength and courage and the dignity with which she bore such suffering for so long. There are also moments when I am frightened that I shall never see her again, but these soon pass and are replaced by a sort of inner calm as I realise that Louise's spirit could never be extinguished – she simply wouldn't allow it!

The boys are growing up now, fine and strong. Both so different. Sam gentle and sensitive, struggling with his uncertainties, unsure of so much. He has a dry, understated sense of humour which he uses to such good effect. Like Louise he has developed a bullshit radar and is quick to pounce. Barney, dark-skinned, tall, athletic and seemingly successful in all he does. He bears strong resemblance to his sister and shares her temper and her talent for language. Last week he went with his sixth form to visit Leeds University. Next year he has resolved to take his place there to study German. In so many ways things have come full circle. In October 2000 we shall once more be driving over the Pennines with Uncle Chris and a bag of oranges – what larks! Louise loved her brothers dearly and would have loved to watch them growing to manhood as I have done. Yes, I'm proud of them both, but Louise was the closest, perhaps because she was my daughter, or was it because she suffered so much – probably a bit of both.

She would have been twenty-eight years old this year, probably married by now and working abroad, she always wanted to work abroad and seemed at her happiest when speaking foreign languages or visiting Germany. I try to visualise her as she would be today. Self-assured, successful, happy? I'll never know. But of some things I'm certain. She would never have lost the child in her, she would still be a dreamer, a seeker of the truth, suspicious of those in authority and mystified by those who seek power for power's sake. I shall never forget her laughter on the day Diana came to open her hospice. The 'hats' and 'suits' really were a great source of amusement to her. Louise would never have become one of those, she was simply too irreverent, too different.

If Louise has left a legacy it is that she irrevocably changed us all probably for the better. She was an inspiration, an example of integrity and courage. We watched her spirit rise above her terrible physical and mental suffering until in the end she had become almost angelic. I often think of her offering to pray for Father Fred on the day of her anointing, and I think I understand better the nature of God. In her short life she touched and inspired so many people, from the terminally ill young Muslim boy she helped to nurse at Christie to the Princess of Wales whose own life was so tragically cut short. Wherever Louise went she was a shining example of courage in the face of terrible adversity. Yes, she was a fine example of all that is best about humanity but what I remember most of all was her laughter and her great love and concern for those around her. Like Diana she made people feel special, and I think that this more than anything else summed up Louise. I can clearly hear her voice as she looked up at me through reddened eyes having been told that she had cancer.

'Are you all right, Daddy?' she said.

She was to repeat this many times during her long battle with cancer and I was never able to proffer a proper response. Seven years later I still haven't thought of an answer. Am I all right? Well, sort of, Louise. Are you?